SAMPFORD PEVERELL

The Village, Church, Chapels and Rectories

From Saxon 'Vill' to 20th Century Village;
the history of Sampford Peverell and its
ecclesiastical buildings

Edited by Charles Scott-Fox

GW00538027

A Sampford Peverell Society publication

Published by
Charles Scott-Fox

ISBN: 0-9547013-2-1

LOTTERY FUNDED

Printed by
Short Run Press Ltd

CONTENTS

List of illustrations

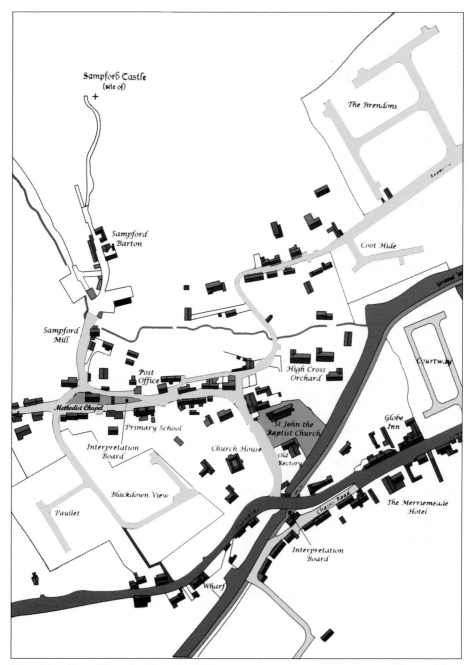

Map of the village of Sampford Peverell - 2005   *(Richard Alford)*

Acknowledgements

Some twenty years ago, taking advantage of some original research by the late Anne Church, I produced a small booklet for the Parochial Church Council outlining the history of the village of Sampford Peverell, the Parish Church and the Old Rectory. I was well aware that this booklet now needed to be updated and to include other ecclesiastical buildings, so when invited by the Chairman of the Sampford Peverell Society to contribute to their first publication, which he wanted to provide an historical introduction for the village and its Church and Chapels, I was honoured and delighted to accept. At about the same time my fellow contributors to this volume had volunteered their services and kindly agreed to my suggestions for their contributions. Val Weller's and Catherine McMurtry's chapters describing the 'Chapels' and the 'Rectories', and the maps and photographs collated by Louise Clunies-Ross to illustrate our text, provide ample proof of their painstaking research and dedication to this project. With the invaluable support and critique of Peter Bowers and with contributions and helpful suggestions from Simon Bartlett and many others in the community, it is hoped that together we have established as complete and up to date a history of this village and its ecclesiastical buildings as is possible.

Although each of the four chapters is attributed we have all made contributions to the text. As research into one part of our village history has established new ideas and conclusions, inevitably this has led to changes elsewhere. I have indeed been fortunate as Editor to have had such a helpful and co-operative team. I am also very pleased to be able to acknowledge the contributions from Di Cowan for taking up-to-date photographs, to Jenny Holley, Bridget Bernhardt, Mervyn Garland, Greville Jefcoate, Julia Claxton and Roger Greenwood for allowing us to reproduce their pictures, to Roger Thorne for permission to use extracts from his work on the Chapels and not least to Christine Butler for putting it all together in such an attractive format.

Finally on behalf of the Society I would like to acknowledge our gratitude to the Master and Fellows of St John's College, Cambridge, Tiverton Museum, Devon Records Office and the Westcountry Studies Library for permission to reproduce items from their collections and above all to the **Local Heritage Initiative** (administered by the Heritage Lottery Fund) for supporting our objectives and providing the grant that has made production of this book feasible.

Charles Scott-Fox
Ayshford 2007

'At Sampford Peverell - 1873'

Introduction

The Sampford Peverell Society was founded in October 2003 with the aim of researching all aspects of the heritage of the Parish of Sampford Peverell. It was decided from the outset to have separate Research Groups, so that members could participate in those aspects of the heritage that particularly interested them: Archaeology, Natural History, Social History, and Buildings & Industry (this latter group now being amalgamated with the Social History Research Group).

During our first two years, and in addition to the activities of the Research Groups, we set up Project Teams to undertake the specific projects for which we had been fortunate to obtain grant funding from the Local Heritage Initiative. These projects included the production of three walk leaflets, two interpretation boards and a village map, the creation of a database and a web-site, as well as hosting an Open Day at which all our findings to date were on display. With this foundation, and with the membership of 90 at the time of writing, the Society is well placed to embark on its next series of projects of which this book is a key element.

This history of a Devon village and its buildings with religious associations is intended to set the scene and will be the first in a series. As research continues, so more fascinating topics are revealed that may be the subject of future publications. In this way, it is intended that the work of the Society will continue for many years to come, being led by the enthusiasm of the Society's members and by others in the community with an interest in our heritage.

Peter Bowers
Chairman Sampford Peverell Society

Figure 1. Aerial view of Sampford Peverell - circa 1989

(Mervyn Garland)

THE VILLAGE OF SAMPFORD PEVERELL

Sampford Peverell sits on a narrow seam of New Red Sandstone, which runs from Minehead in Somerset on the Bristol Channel coast to the south Devon resort of Torquay. Formed some 280 million years ago from broken rock or breccia, in-filling a valley in the folded sedimentary rocks at a time when this land was an equatorial desert, it is the only source of this material in the British Isles. It can be clearly identified by the distinctive ruby red soil and building stone that is seen in the area. The use of this distinctive red local stone for building, in spite of its unsuitability, is a major factor in the appearance of the Devon and Somerset villages that have been built on this sandstone outcrop.

With known evidence of prehistoric man's activity in this region, particularly in the Lowman Valley where long barrows, flint tools and enclosures have been found, this area was clearly as good a place to settle thousands of years ago as it is today. Within the parish of Sampford Peverell, recent finds of Mesolithic flint tools by Society members provide evidence of nomadic hunters and gatherers of the Middle Stone Age roaming the area, possibly as early as 8000 years ago. Worked flint tools of the first farmers from the New Stone Age or Neolithic period (c.4000-2000 BC) have

also been found[1] and some years ago a late Bronze Age socketed axe head (c.1200-700BC) (Fig. 2) was ploughed up by a local farm worker within the village, which is now in the care of Exeter Museum. Aerial photographs of the parish, taken during the hot dry summers of the late 20th century, give indications of interesting crop marks. These have yet to be investigated, but could point to evidence of early settlements. A Legion of the Roman Army (Legio II Augusta) was known to have been established in Exeter in 50 AD. Remains of Roman military forts have been found at Tiverton (Bolham), Huntsham (Cudmore) and Cullompton (St.Andrews Hill), so it would seem likely that Legionaires were marching through the valleys between these forts during their occupation of the south-west in the second half of the 1st century AD.

Centimetres

Figure 2. Bronze Age axe head (Peter Bowers)

Although it has not been possible to establish its precise origins, it is known that Sampford Peverell was a Saxon settlement or 'vill' known as 'Sanforde'. This name means 'sandy ford' and it is presumed that the ford crossed the stream that flows down the valley behind the Parish Church, through the Recreation Ground and under the road beside the Village Hall. According to Folio 113 of Great Domesday, the Lord of the Manor of Sanforde before the Norman Conquest was Beorhtric, a Saxon Thane who lived in Worcestershire[2]. Legend relates that King Edward the Confessor in about 1052 sent Beorhtric on a mission seeking support from the Count of Flanders. There he met the Count's daughter Matilda, who apparently wished to marry him but she was turned down: she subsequently married William Duke of Normandy and thus in due course became Queen of England and in a position to exact her revenge. History would seem to support this tale for in about 1068 Beorhtric was captured and imprisoned in Winchester where he died. All of his lands were forfeited and many of them, including 'Sanforde', were given to Matilda.

In the 10th and 11th centuries the administration of England was devolved by the King to the shires with Bishops having total authority over all ecclesiastical establishments, including both clerical and lay staff, and Ealdormans[3] being given administrative and judicial responsibility for the rest of society. The shires were in turn subdivided into 'hundreds' or 'wapentakes' to which reference is made in Domesday. By 1066 the secular authority for many of these shires was amalgamated, Devonshire becoming part of Wessex and under the control of Harold Godwineson (killed at the Battle of Hastings) with a Shire-Reeve or Sheriff being appointed as his deputy for the county. The Thanes, who owned or administered the land that formed the hundreds, other than those who were tenants of land owned by the Church, were responsible to the Sheriff for their taxes and most importantly for providing men to support the King in time of war. Sampford Peverell was unusual in being one of only nine 'vills' in Devonshire divided between two hundreds being included in the returns of both Halberton and Tiverton.

The extreme south-western shires remained under Saxon control until 1068 when William's Cornubian campaign extended his authority to Devon and Cornwall. Although some Saxon Thanes swore fealty to the new King and retained parts or all of their former estates, the majority were killed or exiled. In 1086 Domesday records that Sampford Peverell was held by Roger de Bully 'from the King. It paid geld [land tax] for 3.5 hides[4]. There is land for 12 ploughs. In demesne [household of the Lord of the Manor] is 1 plough and 6 slaves: and 20 villans and 8 bordars [manorial tenants occupying individual farms or homesteads within a hamlet] with 9 ploughs. There are 30 acres of meadow and 150 acres of pasture and 80 acres of woodland. Formerly 100s [shillings]; now it is worth £10[5]. The Queen gave it to Roger with his wife.'

During the reign of Henry I (1100-1135) the Manor of Sanforde was granted to William Peverell (or Peveril) of Essex and his sister Matilda. Their father, Ralph Peverell, held the Honour of London and several lordships at the time of the Domesday Survey and their ancestors appear to have been in Britain before the Norman Conquest. They were clearly wealthy and important people holding the manors of Aller Peverell in the Parish of Cullompton and Kerswell in Broadhembury.

Their uncle William owned large estates in Nottingham and Derby and was known as 'Peveril of the Peak'. Towards the end of the reign of Henry I, William and Matilda Peverell enfeoffed [transferred] the Lordship of the Manor of Sanforde together with their other manors to the forebears of their great nephew Hugh and it remained in this branch of their family for a further six generations, latterly in the female line, until 1399 when Sir William Asthorpe died without an heir and the Manor reverted to the King, Henry IV. Tristram Risdon's *Survey of Devon*[6] describes this succession of the Lordship of Sampford Peverell in the 14th century which 'was the ancient inheritance of the Peverells, which began to inhabit in this shire in king Henry the first's days. Some of this noble name were stiled lords of Nottingham and Derby, as our grand antiquary hath it. Thomas, the last of this family, left his lands to his three sisters, Joan, the wife of sir John Wraxall, Margaret, married to sir Elias Cottle, and Dionese, to sir John de la Rivers, knights. After these in the time of king Edward the third, Oliver Dynham held this land.'

Figure 3. Site of Sampford Castle - 2006   *(David Curnow)*

In the mid 13th century the Peverell family replaced the old Saxon Church and built the Castle. In 1605 Risdon described the castle as 'standing very pleasantly on the side of a hill, having underneath it a fair pond or pool, serving both for pleasure and profit.' An earth mound, which is the site of this castle (Fig. 3), can be seen above Sampford Barton Farm beside the North Devon Link Road, but little is known except that it was rebuilt and fortified in 1337 and, having long been in a ruinous state, it was finally demolished in 1775[7]: nothing now remains on the site. During the Lordship of the Peverells the name of the Manor had been changed to Sampford and the suffix Peverell (Peveril in some documents) was added. At some time towards the end of the 13th century the vill of Sampford Peverell was given Borough status, but it never expanded sufficiently to rival Tiverton and by the end of the 18th century it had returned to being a village at the centre of the parish. As a Borough it held two Fairs during the year, the better known taking place on the Monday before the last Wednesday in April. These Fairs were extremely popular (Fig. 4) but declined in the years between the wars and the last was held in 1948.

Sir William Asthorpe was the last of the Lords of the Manor with a Peverell connection and when he died without issue, it reverted to the Crown. In about 1400 Henry IV presented the Manor to his half-brother John Beaufort, the first Earl and subsequently Duke of Somerset: through him it came by hereditary right to his grand-daughter, Margaret Beaufort Countess of Richmond and Derby and the mother of King Henry VII (Fig. 5): her tomb can be seen in Westminster Abbey. She was a truly generous benefactor whose impact on the village remains to this day. During the reigns of Edward IV and Richard III, as the mother of a claimant to the English throne, it is understood that she took refuge from time to time in this remote Devonshire village, probably in the Castle. Following the Tudor victory over Richard III at the Battle of Bosworth Field in 1485, and her son's accession to the throne as Henry VII, she occasionally returned to Sampford Peverell and in 1500 built the house now known

Figure 4. Sampford Fair - circa 1900

*Figure 5. Lady Margaret Beaufort
(St. John's College, Cambridge)*

as the Old Rectory on land adjacent to the Parish Church. Over the years she also provided the necessary funds to enlarge or restore the Parish Churches of both Sampford Peverell and Uplowman. After her death in 1509 she left her house to the Parish but the Lordship once again returned to the Crown and in 1540 the manor was sold by Henry VIII to the Powlett (or Poulett) family of Hinton St.George in Somerset. In 1549 Sampford Peverell was the unwitting cause of an insurrection when a local child was baptised. Peter Belcher in his *Tiverton: A History and Celebration* wrote... 'The bitter disputes between the traditionalist Roman Catholics and the followers of the new Protestant faith led to much blood-shed throughout England in the 16th century, affecting everyone from the royal court down to the humblest of men. The fires of controversy were further fuelled on Whit Sunday 1549 with the introduction of the Common Prayer Book. For the first time the congregation was able to hear the order of service in English as opposed to Latin. Locally, matters came to a head with the baptism of a child in Sampford Peverell, some five miles to the east of Tiverton. As often happens, there was a split between the generations; the oldest members of the family wanting the traditional Catholic service, their younger relatives preferring the Protestant version. Such was the animosity that the Catholic faction withdrew to Cranmore Castle [south of Tiverton and known locally as 'Shrinkhills'] where they were summarily dealt with by a detachment of the King's army. Although some were taken prisoner, many were executed for "heretical" actions'. The Lordship remained with the Powlett family until their estate was broken up and sold in 1806. During this time the Borough of Sampford Peverell declined in line with other rural communities so that by 1741 there were no more than 150 families living in the village. It was the start of construction of the Grand Western Canal[8] that was to temporarily revive fortunes. Although originally conceived in 1769 as a means of bringing coal from South Wales to Exeter without the risk of shipwreck around the coast of Cornwall, the lack of adequate financial backing delayed the start of construction until 1810. The route of the canal cut through the centre of the village of Sampford Peverell, separating Higher Town from Lower Town. As the map of 1844 (Fig. 6) clearly shows, the Turnpike was diverted from its original route, along what is now Chains Road, to cross the canal below the Old Rectory before rejoining its original line to Batten's Cross. The canal also removed most of the Rectory garden, its stable block and rear east wing and several houses in Lower Town. Two properties,

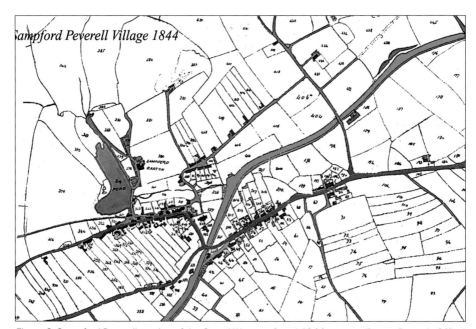

Figure 6. Sampford Peverell section of the Grand Western Canal 1844   *(Devon Records Office)*

one at the top of the hill in Lower Town and one in Chains Road, had to be partially rebuilt to allow for the line of the canal and its towpath. However, the foundations of the old Gatehouse for the village, now 1 Chains Road, remain although the road that it guarded, which gave access to Higher Town, no longer exists. The Act of 1811, which had amended the route of the canal, required the 'Company within three years to either purchase or build some other suitable dwelling as parsonage house in lieu'[9]. However the company was permanently in debt and it was not until 1841 that the new Rectory, which is now known as Church House, was built and handed over to the Parish. The Old Rectory became the property of the Canal Company; after a few years, when it was let as two separate properties, it was given to a charitable trust to be used as the first National School in the Parish.

Work had started on the Sampford Peverell section in 1813 but was not completed until the following year. The canal was opened for barge traffic from Tiverton to Lowdwells on 25th August 1814. The extension for tub boats from Lowdwells to Taunton, which utilised inclined planes and lifts to reduce water loss, was started in 1831 and completed in June 1838. Over the succeeding six years traffic, which previously had been restricted to lime and road-stone between Canonsleigh and Tiverton, steadily increased with a wide variety of cargo including coal from South Wales for which the project had originally been conceived. The peak of toll income was in 1844 but in 1842 the Bristol & Exeter Railway had reached Taunton, and by 1848 the completed line to Exeter had a spur to Tiverton. An agreement between the canal and railway companies had given the railway the right to carry coal, leaving the canal to transport stone and lime, but local traders switched virtually all their trade to the railway, precipitating a steady decline in canal revenues. However the railway company was also losing money, by continually having to undercut canal tolls, and by 1853 both companies were ready to settle. Initially the canal was transferred to the railway company under a ten year lease at £2000/year; but in the early 1860s further negotiations resulted in agreement to petition for an Act of Parliament, to authorise the sale of the Canal Company to the Bristol & Exeter Railway Company for £30,000, which came into law in July 1864. The Lowdwells to Taunton section was closed in 1867 but the Tiverton to Lowdwells length continued transporting lime and stone for a further 60 years.

In 1925 all commercial traffic ceased and maintenance was subsequently kept to a minimum resulting in excessive weed and lily growth and silting. In 1948 the canal, by then being owned by the Great Western Railway Company, was nationalised and in due course was passed to the newly established British Waterways Board. In 1962 it was formally closed to navigation and nine years later was given to Devon County Council as a recreational facility. In 1991 the canal was made a Conservation Area and the Council initiated a progressive programme of dredging and improvement to the canal bank and towpath. In addition to its traditional recreational and coarse fishing activities this remaining 11.5 mile stretch of the Grand Western Canal has now been formally recognised as a Local Nature Reserve (Fig. 7) and the towpath incorporated into the National Cycle Network.

Figure 7. Grand Western Canal - Conservation area and Nature Reserve   *(Di Cowan)*

Until the latter part of the 20th century, the local economy was primarily dependant on farming and associated light industries. According to the 1821 census, 131 of the 174 families in the parish were engaged in agriculture. There had also been a thriving weaving industry with many homes having their own looms to produce clothing for local use but, within a period of only a few years, this work was transferred to mills in nearby Tiverton and Uffculme, where new machinery could produce clothing more efficiently and at a lower cost. By 1822, there were only a few weavers left in the parish[10] and the effect of this sudden loss of trade on these vulnerable local economies must have been quite severe. For a time the leather industry, which had been a feature of village life since at least the beginning of the 17th century, had greater success. By 1819 the tannery, which was situated on the eastern side of the Globe Inn, had grown into a substantial business being capable of tanning upwards of 50 hides a week[11]. However by 1841 advances in technology had made the production processes used by small village tanneries uneconomic, and the business was forced to close. The old tannery was subsequently converted and extended to become the East Devon County School, a private school for boys. In 1907, the premises were acquired for St Boniface's Home for Boys, a Church of England Home for Waifs and Strays, which accommodated up to 70 boys from age seven to fourteen. The Home was closed in 1952[12] and the site was redeveloped as part of Court Way.

Figure 8. Pretty Bench Quarry - circa 1982

Figure 9. Higher Town - circa 1910

There were several small quarries to the north of the village producing brecchia, a combination of New Red Sandstone and Limestone, primarily for building. Both these materials were also used to produce lime for fertiliser and mortar in the lime-kilns, though that produced from the Sampford Sandstone was markedly inferior. The remains of some of these quarries and kilns can be seen on Connigar Hill, off the road to Whitnage near Mount Pleasant and also beside the canal to the north of Burlescombe, but the local 'Pretty Bench' quarry (Fig. 8) was destroyed during construction of the North Devon Link Road. During the 19th century these quarries were becoming depleted and, with improved methods of transport, other building materials were brought in, but lime production continued well into the 20th century.

The only industry of significant size to be established in the village in the 19th century was the R.S. Norrish and Sons dairy in Chains Road[13]. This family business, operated on traditional lines, flourished until the Second World War when it was bought out. After the war the building was converted into an animal feed mill; when that closed it was used as a carpet warehouse and in the 1990s as a joinery. The site has now been re-developed for housing. In 1977 a company known as Westward Packaging was established near Batten's Cross to manufacture cardboard cartons. In 1995 it was acquired by a Danish firm and two years later transferred to new premises in Burlescombe; this site has also been re-developed for housing.

All of the above can only confirm that between 1850 and the 1990s Sampford Peverell was a thriving community (Fig. 9 and 10) supporting a variety of rural industries, which perforce were changing with the advances of the industrial and

Figure 10. Lower Town - circa 1930

technological age. Until the First World War all of one's daily needs could be met within the village, which had grist mills, a smithy, a bakery, several inns and shops selling a variety of essential goods. Between the wars these local services fell into a gradual decline as people became accustomed to travelling to nearby towns to make their purchases but even in the 1990s there were still two public houses, four shops, a Doctor's Surgery and a garage. Unfortunately this decline accelerated after the end of the century and in 2006 only the Globe Inn, the village Post Office and surgery survived. However it is hoped that a second shop will be built on the old garage site and the Merriemeade has since re-opened to provide some restoration in the level of services for the local community. Other facilities in the wider parish include a hotel, guest house, bed and breakfast and self-catering accommodation, hair-dressing salon, farm shop, caravan site, golf driving range and a nationally recognised specialist shrub nursery.

In 1857 the Reverend George William Rossiter Ireland had been appointed as Rector of Sampford Peverell with Uplowman. He was an extremely wealthy man and over the succeeding twenty-five years used much of his fortune for an extensive rebuilding and restoration of the Parish Church of St. John the Baptist. In 1874 he extended this generosity to the children of the village by providing the land and £750 to build the Church of England Primary School building that can be seen opposite the Post Office in Higher Town.

Figure 11. The Great Pond and causeway leading to Sampford Barton - circa 1905

The 20th century has brought considerable change to the village. The Great Pond (Fig. 11) that had been a major feature of the village since the middle ages, was drained, leaving only the old mill as evidence of its existence. Between 1919 and 1939 there was a steady decline and many of the older thatched properties, including the old Bakery and a most attractive house at the junction of Higher Town and Barton Lane, were burnt down. One of the houses that has been lost achieved considerable notoriety in the early 19th century when it was featured in the Reverend Caleb Colton's *Narrative of the Sampford Ghost*.[14] At the time he was the Sampford Peverell Curate but living in Tiverton and in April 1810 had been asked by one of his parishioners, Mr John Chave, whose house was apparently haunted and whose family and servants were being subjected to the often violent attacks of a ghost or poltergeist, to investigate these events. Both the Reverend Colton and the Governor of Exeter Prison, called in as an independent witness, heard strange noises and were assaulted but local opinion suggested that John Chave was faking these activities to enable him to purchase the property cheaply. Although never proven the 'ghost' disappeared and it was later discovered that the house had passages between the walls, which might have given him the opportunity to create this apparition.

The continuing drift of the population out of the country and into the towns continued after the Second World War and Sampford Peverell was no exception. At its lowest point there were barely 600 electors but to-day, thanks in part to modern communications and in part to society's desire to enjoy rural life, the village is expanding once again with development of the few remaining industrial sites and some of the immediately adjacent green fields. Most of this expansion must be attributed to the impact of the M5 Motorway, the North Devon Link Road and Tiverton Parkway Station, each of which provides ready access for commuters from the village to Exeter and Taunton and by train or motorway to London and the rest of the country. In particular the building of the North Devon Link Road, which replaced the old A361 from its junction with the A38 at Waterloo Cross through Sampford Peverell and Halberton to Tiverton, had a dramatic impact on these two villages as through traffic was virtually eliminated. Especially in the holiday season the continuous stream of caravans and heavy goods vehicles made life in Lower Town and Turnpike a nightmare. Now Sampford Peverell is once again an attractive place to live and with well over 1000 electors the natural cycle in the population of the village, which can be traced through the ages from Saxon times to the present day, has risen to a level that even exceeds the peaks of the early 19th century. Evidence of this cycle is particularly clear in the building and restoration of the Parish Church. Here too can be noted the connection with the noble and landed families that once formed part of this community and with the Beaufort and Ireland families to whose generosity the Parish is indebted to this day.

1. Details of these finds are held in the Sites and Monuments Register at County Hall, Exeter

2. The names and spellings used here are taken from the official Public Record Office reproduction and translation to celebrate Domesday's 900th anniversary produced by Alecto Publications in 1986. The Exon Domesday, the only surviving individual County record, which is held by the Cathedral, shows minor differences to both the Exchequer version based on the 1873 reproduction and interpretation and to this latest translation. The Exon text states 'Roger de Busle has a manor called Sanforda which Bristritius held on the day on which king Edward was alive and dead, and it rendered geld for three hides and a half. These can be ploughed by twelve ploughs. Of these Roger has in demesne one hide and a half, and half a ferling, and one plough, and the villeins have two hides less half a ferling and eight ploughs. There Roger has twenty villeins, and eight bordars, and six serfs, and eight swine, and eightyfour sheep, and fifty goats, and eighty acres of wood, and thirty acres of meadow, and a hundred and fifty acres of pasture. And it is worth [returns] by the year ten pounds, and it was worth a hundred shillings when he received it. Queen Matilda gave this manor to Roger de Busle with his wife.'

The differences between these three versions of the 11th century text are: Roger de Busle is de Busli in the Exchequer Domesday which is translated by Alecto as de Bully; Sanforda is Sanforde (Alecto deliberately uses the modern equivalent of Sampford Peverell in its translation); and the Saxon Thane Bristritius is Bricgric in the actual Domesday text but written Brictric in the Exchequer Domesday and translated to Beorhtric by Alecto.

3. The Old English title of Ealdorman (*Ealdor*, lord + *mann*, man) survived the Conquest but by the late 11th century had been replaced by the Norman *Jarl* - a nobleman or commander. In 1066 there were four main divisions of the kingdom with Ealdormans having responsibility for Wessex, Mercia, East Anglia and Northumbria. Following the Conquest these administrative areas were reduced in size, reverting to the shires.

4. The 'hide' had several meanings at this time but is described in the OED as the extent of land that can be tilled by one plough in a year which may be said to equate to 100 acres.

5. This is a very substantial assessment only exceeded by the holdings in towns such as Bampton (£18) but notably has not changed from the pre-Conquest tax payable to Edward the Confessor.

6. *The Chorographical Description of Survey of the County of Devon* was written by Tristram Risdon in

1605 but the manuscript was not published until 1811. Re-printed by Porcupines, Barnstaple in 1970 from which this and subsequent quotations on page 20 are taken.

7. Although never seriously defended it is believed to have been partially demolished by Parliamentarians during their campaign to capture the City of Exeter in 1646.

8. For full details of the history of this canal see *The Grand Western Canal* by Helen Harris; David & Charles 1973

9. Ibid: p.39.

10. *Magna Britannia- Volume VI* (Devonshire Part II) by Rev Daniel Lysons and Samuel Lysons, Thomas Cadell, London, 1822: p.432-433

11. Sherborne Mercury 23.08.1819. The tanning process also involved the use of lime and the Sampford Peverell premises had 3 lime pits.

12. www.hiddenlives.org.uk

13. *The Transition from Tradition to Technology: A History of the Dairy Industry in Devon* by Peter Sainsbury, P.T.Sainsbury 1991:p.69-70

14. *Ghosts of Devon* by Peter Underwood, Bossiney Books 1982, p.82

THE PARISH CHURCH OF SAINT JOHN THE BAPTIST

The Parish Church of Sampford Peverell occupies a key site on a small knoll between Higher Town and Lower Town (Fig. 12). Its dominance today is lessened by development and the intrusion of the Grand Western Canal into the adjacent former Rectory garden, but it still can be clearly seen from the surrounding countryside, the M5 and the North Devon Link Road.

Figure 12. Aerial view of the Parish Church of Saint John the Baptist - circa 1980

The Nave and Chancel of the existing church was constructed on the site of a Saxon or Norman building of which the only surviving relic is the Norman Font. It was probably built by Sir Hugh Peverell, Knight and Lord of the Manor of Sanforde 1241-1296 and a Crusader under Richard of Cornwall, the brother of Henry III. The building was made mostly of the local red Sampford Sandstone and consisted of a Nave and Chancel under a continuous roof with a Tower and wooden Spire being added later. It was dedicated to Saint John the Baptist by the Bishop of Devon and Cornwall on the Wednesday after the Feast of Saint Nicholas, 10th December 1259. During a week-long tour of East Devon Bishop Bronescombe dedicated the Churches of Broadhembury, Ottery St. Mary, Dunkeswell, Payhembury, Sheldon, Kentisbeare and Sampford Peverell. The seven hundredth anniversary of this unique event was commemorated in 1959 by a service of thanksgiving at Ottery St. Mary led by the Bishop of Exeter, Bishop Robert Mortimer and attended by representatives of the seven parishes. On 12th April 1318, the Church at Sampford Peverell[1] was

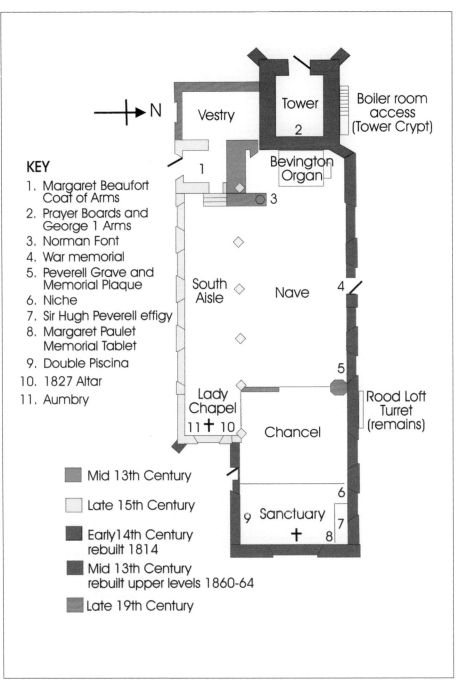

N

KEY

1. Margaret Beaufort
   Coat of Arms
2. Prayer Boards and
   George 1 Arms
3. Norman Font
4. War memorial
5. Peverell Grave and
   Memorial Plaque
6. Niche
7. Sir Hugh Peverell effigy
8. Margaret Paulet
   Memorial Tablet
9. Double Piscina
10. 1827 Altar
11. Aumbry

Vestry

Tower
2

Boiler room
access
(Tower Crypt)

Bevington
Organ

1

3

South
Aisle

Nave

4

5

Lady
Chapel

11 ✝ 10

Chancel

Rood Loft
Turret
(remains)

6

9 Sanctuary
       ✝   7
          8

Mid 13th Century

Late 15th Century

Early14th Century
rebuilt 1814

Mid 13th Century
rebuilt upper levels 1860-64

Late 19th Century

Figure 13. Plan of Saint John the Baptist Church   *(Ron Holmes)*

rededicated by Bishop Stapleton. Records provide no explanation and it can only be assumed that either the Church had been desecrated in some way or that the Bishop was dedicating the addition of the Tower and Spire.

Pevsner[2] describes this church as being 'uncommonly instructive architecturally', which indeed it is, being one of very few small parish churches of the mid-13th century to have survived with most of its original form intact (Fig. 13). When first constructed it was a simple rectangular building, measuring approximately 30 x 8.5 metres externally, and with walls that were well in excess of a metre thick at their base. The east window has 'three lancets under a hoodmould' and the surviving two Chancel and four of the five north Nave wall double lancet lights 'have tall nook shafts towards the interior with typically Early English moulded capitals. The shafts rest on a roll-moulded string course[3] which is carried around the North Door. The window arches are low', with their 13th century provenance being well established by the elementary style of tracery, which may be compared to the more elaborate Perpendicular windows of the late 15th century South Aisle. The fifth window, at the western end of the north wall of the Nave, is a very simple triple lancet light with no tracery or shafts and a flat arch. (For a description of the glazing see Appendix 2.)

Figure 14. Double Piscina - South wall of the Sanctuary (Di Cowan)

Built into the south wall of the Sanctuary is a 'beautiful double Piscina (Fig. 14) of the 13th century with paired arches, trefoil headed with shafts and mouldings corresponding with the nook shafts in the windows. On the north side there is an Aumbry with a pair of trefoil headed arches rebated for a door'.[4] Two of the 13th century entrances remain; a very simple low Priest's door that leads through the south wall directly into the Chancel and the North Door (Fig. 15), formerly the principal entrance to the Nave from the village, 'with a very flat arch on [nook] shafts with shaft rings'. Built of Thorverton stone with a hoodmould it is noted as being one of the most attractive Early English architectural features of this building. It would be expected that this Church was also provided with a West Door, but the addition of the Tower and its subsequent rebuilding in the early 19th century means that this can only be assumption based on similar buildings of the period.

Although substantially restored in 1815 the well-built low Tower retains most of its early 14th century features, allowing Pevsner to give a firm attribution and to add his

Figure 15. Nave North Door   *(Di Cowan)*   *Figure 16. Tower West Door*   *(Di Cowan)*

support for Bishop Stapleton's visit in 1318 being to dedicate this addition to the Church. The Tower was constructed with 'big blocks of reddish ashlar with diagonal buttresses' and provided with four twin lancet 'bell openings with simple plate tracery'. There is no evidence of a stair turret and it must be assumed that access to the roof, and the shingled Spire that originally crowned this Church, has always been by internal ladders. It has three stages with diagonal buttresses and an embattled parapet with corner pinnacles. The clock face, added in the late 19th century, has a cusped hoodmould. The West Door is an unusual two centred arch, with a moulded surround containing a square headed door with fanlight above with cusped tracery (Fig. 16). There are indications that there was an arched opening from the Nave into the base of the Tower, but the higher ground into which this end of the Church was built would have required several steps. However, even if they had survived the rebuilding of the Tower in the early 19th century, any remaining evidence was lost when the internal tower wall was plastered and the floor levelled prior to the installation of the Organ in 1870.

There were no further additions to the Church until the end of the 15th century when Lady Margaret Beaufort paid for the building of the South Aisle. In 1498 the south wall of the Nave and part of the Chancel were removed and replaced by a 5-bay Beerstone arcade of 'tall Type A piers with capitals only to the shafts' (Fig. 17). The new Aisle, which with its accompanying South Porch measures approximately 22 x

4 metres, has 'a decorative west gable with quatrefoil panelling, and five three light Perpendicular windows'. Originally its south wall was embattled with quatrefoil pierced panels but this parapet was removed, probably as part of the general repairs in the early 19th century, and the only surviving panel is the one that was installed in the west gable when the Vestry was added in 1870. The rising ground on which this Church was built also created problems for access from this new Aisle to the Porch; four steep steps being needed to come from the floor of the Church to the ground level of the Porch.

In the 18th century Sampford Peverell was noted for its 'magnificent' Rood Screen and Loft. Since the only evidence relates to its removal in 1826, it is clearly impossible to provide an accurate date for this feature, but it seems likely to have been contemporary with the Aisle. The Loft was accessed from a Rood Turret, which was removed in the reconstruction of the north wall in 1863-64, leaving a wide buttress on the junction of Nave and Chancel as the only evidence of its existence.

Figure 17. Church interior east - Nave, Chancel and South Aisle arcade   *(Di Cowan)*

Margaret Beaufort's involvement in all of this work is commemorated by her Coat of Arms inside the Porch (Fig. 18); they can also be seen over the door of the house that she built in 1500, which is now known as the Old Rectory. In 1605 Risdon recorded that her generosity was featured in one of the Aisle windows by 'the arms of England with the arms of the earl of Derby, were not long since to be seen, with this underwritten in the glass "Mater Regis et Thome comitis Derbie mariti ejusden Margaret' [5]. She may also have been responsible for the building of a Cross that is known to have stood on the high ground to the west of the Church. Probably taken down during the Cromwellian period [1649-1660], it had certainly been removed by 1700. The Cross is remembered to this day by the names of the houses built opposite the site, High Cross House and Cross Hill Cottage. The Village Stocks were originally sited here, but were transferred to the Churchyard by the Reverend Rossiter Ireland in the late 1800s. In the 1970s they were moved to Coldharbour Mill in Uffculme but have now been returned on permanent loan to the Sampford Peverell Society.

Figure 18. Beaufort Coat of Arms (Di Cowan)

During the 18th century the living was in plurality with Uplowman (see Appendix 1), where the Rector lived and where the majority of services were held. In common with most of the rest of England, church life was at a low ebb and the Church suffered from considerable neglect. Although for part of the time the Parish had a Curate, he lived in Tiverton and it seems little was done to maintain the fabric. In 1741 the Reverend Bertie Henley, in answer to a questionnaire from the Bishop, wrote that of the 150 families in the village 'whereof 3 are Dissenters of that sort who go under ye denomination of Presbyterian' that there were 30 Communicants at Easter, and that the Holy Sacrament of the Lord's Supper was celebrated four times in the year! By the end of the century the Church was in such poor repair and the roof leaked so badly that services could no longer be held there. The Tower with its shingled Spire was clearly in an even more dangerous state for when, in about 1814, limited funds became available, presumably compensation from the Canal Company, it was decided that this must have priority. Accordingly the Tower was rebuilt and this is commemorated by a weather worn plaque over the West Door. 'This tower was erected in 1815, replacing the original one built in Early English style with a spire.' Six years later a Vestry meeting was held to decide whether the rest of the Church was worth restoring or whether it should be pulled down and rebuilt. It was decided to repair the Church and some work appears to have been done over the next few years as records state that the Rood Loft (and Screen) was removed in 1826.

When the Reverend George William Rossiter Ireland became Rector of Sampford Peverell in 1857 he found the Church in a poor state and spent the next 13 years restoring and 'improving' it. He was a man with considerable means and paid for nearly all of the work himself. However he was determined that both his contemporaries and his successors should be reminded of his munificence, wherever they might be in the building, for there are no less than thirteen different tablets and inscriptions in the Church giving his name as benefactor and donor. As it states

Figure 19. Church interior west - Nave, South Aisle and Organ   *(Di Cowan)*

on one of these tablets 'The Nave and Aisle, having fallen into grievous decay, was completely restored, re-seated and the north wall rebuilt in strict conformity with the originals by the joint subscription of the Rector and parishioners in the year of Our Lord 1863–1864, Reverend George William Rossiter Ireland LLD Rector, John Beedle, Wm Payne, Churchwardens.' However to his credit it is this 'strict conformity with the original', which Rossiter Ireland and his architect Ashworth had demanded, that has enabled Sampford Peverell to retain its status as a supreme example of mid-13th century provincial architecture (Fig. 19). The walls of the Chancel, the Nave below its string course and the north door with its surrounding stonework, are almost certainly wholly original. Above the string course it can only be conjecture as to how much was taken down to be rebuilt but some of the Thorverton stone window shafts are missing or misplaced and it seems likely that the Nave wall was rebuilt above window sill level. There are no tablets in the Aisle or Porch to inform us of Rossiter Ireland's involvement in this part of the Church so it is assumed that the repairs undertaken in 1826 were satisfactory. Clearly the roof has been totally restored with 19th century arch-braced trusses and boarded backs. In the Nave the trusses spring from moulded Beerstone corbels, whereas those in the Chancel have corbels carved with stiff leafed foliage. The Chancel roof also has single sets of wind-braces. Most of the windows were filled with stained glass by the well-known Victorian artist Westlake (for a detailed description of these and the two Aisle windows left plain at the time but subsequently glazed see Appendix 2). All of the doors were severely decayed and replaced with 19th century reproductions. The only new construction that Rossiter

Ireland commissioned was the small lean-to Vestry, with its tiny fireplace and tall chimney, which was added in the south-west corner and accessed from the Porch (Fig.20). A safe was mounted in the fireplace in the 1990s.

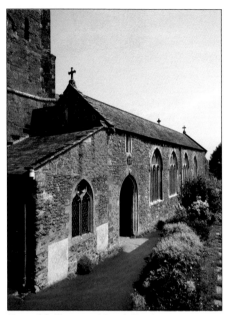

Figure 20. Vestry and South Porch
(Di Cowan)

The Parish owes so much to this extraordinarily generous man and his wife and the quality of the work that he and his architect required. As a result there was little work, other than routine maintenance, that was needed to keep the Church in good order for over a century. In 1959 central heating was installed, the Sanctuary was enlarged internally, enabling the celebrant to stand behind the Altar to face the congregation, and the High Altar, which had been made in 1827, was lengthened. In 1984 the Churchwardens created a Lady Chapel at the east end of the Aisle. Mr Ken Keitch, the People's Warden at the time, restored the Altar to its original size and it was placed beneath the Aisle east window. He built a new High Altar, which together with the Lady Chapel, was consecrated by Bishop Westall of Crediton. The most recent restoration of the fabric was carried out in the 1990s; this included a new lead roof for the Tower and valley between Nave and Aisle, re-pointing of all east, north and west facing walls including the Tower, replacement of all iron glazing bars with stainless steel and restoration of decaying pillars in the Aisle east window.

The Ring of Bells and Tower Clock

The Tower carries a ring of six bells. The inscriptions and other details are given in Appendix 3. The history of the bells, prior to their recasting in 1761, is obscure. In 1553 the Inventory of Church Goods, made under Edward VI, states that there were five bells in Sampford Peverell Church Tower. Most churches at that time had only three or four so Sampford Peverell was unusually well endowed. In 1761 these five bells were recast by Thomas Bilbie of Cullompton. The family had started bell founding at Chewstoke in Somerset and Thomas Bilbie moved to Cullompton to fill the space in Devon bell founding left by the closure of the Exeter Foundry in the late 1720s. The new ring of five included a Tenor Bell of about 15 hundredweight, which by 1863 had cracked and was again recast by George Mears of Whitechapel.

In 1869 Rossiter Ireland, who had already shown his interest in the bells with the recasting of the old Tenor, donated a new heavier Tenor in memory of his sister. This new bell was about a ton in weight and sounded the note E Flat; this made it necessary to lower the note of the third bell by a semitone to bring the ring into the new key. This was achieved without recasting and both this bell and the fourth show the marks of very heavy tuning with a chisel or hammer. The bell frame was renewed at the same time to accommodate the enlarged ring. The bells were re-hung in 1948 by Taylor's of Loughborough (Fig.21). The frame was reinforced with tie-bolts and angle plates and at the same time the cannons on the heads of the bells were removed and the bells hung in cast-iron headstocks. Sampford Peverell has a long history of bell-ringing and is frequently visited by ringers from other parishes for the experience. Mary Coyle, daughter of the Reverend Matthew Coyle (Rector 1943-1962) recalled that on New Year's Eve 'the bell-ringers had a traditional Bell-ringers Supper of pre-prepared foods: beef, ham, pickles, beer to drink' all provided by the Parish. 'They then rang in the New Year, often watched by villagers at the bell-tower door.'

The Clock was installed by Gillett & Bland of Croydon in 1870. It is a 'flat-bed' movement, the frame being over four feet long, with quarter chimes [a version of the Westminster quarters but now silenced] and hour strike with one dial on the

Figure 21. The Sampford Peverell Ring of Bells rehung by Taylor's of Loughborough - 1948 (Tiverton Museum)

south face. The pendulum beats 40 to the minute, driven by a six-legged gravity escapement, and is wound by hand every 60 hours.

Interior fittings and Monuments

Although the North Door can still be opened (the Chancel Door is never used), visitors usually enter the Church through the South Porch where they are immediately confronted by the Coat of Arms of Margaret Beaufort. On the left is the entrance to the Vestry and on the right a small flight of steps that leads down into the South Aisle. Furniture and fittings are mostly from the nineteenth century renovation. A Gothic style Reredos above the Altar has a central panel featuring the Good Samaritan. The oak Communion Rail is particularly attractive with twisted wrought-iron standards and repoussé brackets. The Chancel candelabrum is another notable wrought-iron feature being complemented by those fitted to the pews throughout the main body of the Church. The Church had no other means of illumination until the 1930s, when electricity became available, and candles were essential for the congregation to read their prayer books and hymnals. The candelabra are still used for festivals and other special services, being particularly popular for weddings. Separating Chancel and Nave is a low Salcombe stone screen, which in 1870 almost totally enclosed the Chancel but now only survives on the south side. On the north side, built into the Chancel wall, is the Pulpit of identical stone and similar Early English styling (Fig. 22). Apart from a few loose chairs

Figure 22. Pulpit   *(Di Cowan)*

the Chancel was totally bare until choir stalls were installed in the late 20th century. The stall on the north side was made by Ken Keitch and the Bishop's and Rector's stalls and the south frontal were made by the local cabinet-maker Mark Williams. The pews are early Victorian, being purchased second-hand by Rossiter Ireland from an unknown church or chapel; originally painted black, they were restored to their natural wood finish in 1989. By the entrance door is the Norman Beerstone Drum Font (Fig. 23), the only surviving relic of the original church on this site. In 1846 there was a modern font, the bowl of this old Norman Font being used to

Figure 23. Norman Font   *(Di Cowan)*   *Figure 24. Bevington Organ*   *(Di Cowan)*

catch the drip of water from the roof of the Old Rectory. The bowl was re-united with its shaft and installed at the back of the Church by Rossiter Ireland in 1862. KM Clark wrote that it was 'originally of star design but re-tooled until it has entirely lost its character.'[6] Below the bowl the saltire and bead band is 12th century but the shaft is later and the base Victorian.

Behind the Font in the recess of the internal Tower wall is the Bevington Organ (Fig. 24). Installed by Rossiter Ireland in 1870, this notable instrument was dismantled and re-built with two new pipes by Michael Farley of Budleigh in 1989. Prior to the fitting of an electric pump the organ was operated by hand bellows. With Matins, Evensong and a Sunday School service every Sunday there was a roster of men and boys allocated to the task of ensuring that there was sufficient air pressure on the gauge for the organist to produce the music for the appropriate hymns, psalms and responses. Members of the congregation in those days recalled that on occasions there was silence or a petering out as the lack of air pressure brought the service to a standstill. The bellows boy, bored by the sermon or just too tired to stay awake, would be woken by the organist banging the keyboard or kicked into action by an irate Churchwarden and the service would resume.

The oldest monument is undoubtedly the very worn and damaged Beerstone effigy in the north-east corner of the Sanctuary (Fig. 25). Originally placed in the Nave, this soft stone monument could be touched or sat on by any passer-by and became badly worn as a result. It is a somewhat mutilated figure in plate armour wearing a helmet and long tunic. On his left arm he carries a shield and his right is in the act of drawing his sword. It is generally accepted that this represents Sir Hugh Peverell Kt, who was Patron of the Church in 1278. As part of the restoration in 1863 all of the floors were re-tiled and many bodies, including four members of the Peverell

Figure 25. Effigy of Sir Hugh Peverell   *(Di Cowan)*

family, were discovered under the Nave. They were all recorded, re-interred and the vaults closed in. The stone above the Peverell vault was inscribed 'Grave of the Peverells' together with a brass plaque on the adjacent north wall 'Beneath this spot rests in death the body of Sir Hugh Peverell Knight, munificent founder of this Church about the year of Our Lord 1200 [sic] together with the bodies of three other members of the ancient and honourable family of Peverell former Lords of the Manor. The remains were discovered in 1863 by the Rector the Revd George W. R. Ireland, who reverently re-interred them and put up this brass to their memory.' The arms on this plaque (Fig. 26) are stated to be those of Sir Hugh Peverell Kt. the head of the Devon Peverell family but according to Risdon they are those of the Nottingham branch. As the Devon Peverells had extensive estates in Cornwall it has also been suggested that members of this family could have been buried there and that the effigy might represent Sir Elias Cottle Kt, Patron in 1324, who had inherited the Sampford estate when he married the heiress daughter of Sir Hugh Peverell. However as Risdon also noted 'there was also to be seen the armed proportion of one of the Peverells, cut cross-legged in stone, who bare in a field azure, three garbes argent, a chief or, which were in divers of the windows'[7] so unless some new evidence comes to light the weight of opinion seems to rest with Rossiter Ireland's inscription and the Peverell name.

There is no such controversy over the Powlett [Poulett] memorial on the east wall.

She was the daughter and heiress of Anthony Harvey Esquire of Columb St. John and was married to Sir Amias Powlett Kt. whose father Sir Hugh Powlett Kt. had purchased the Lordship in 1540. Sir Amias was a devoted and loyal servant of Elizabeth I serving as her Ambassador to France and in 1585 as the custodian of Mary Queen of Scots at Tutbury and Chartley; he was subsequently on the commission for her trial at Fotheringay. Cresswell believed 'that he was almost too conscientious for the spirit of the times; he stoutly resisted any plans for the assignation (sic) of Mary whilst she was in his charge and had no credit for his honesty.' Sir Amias died in 1588 and his wife fourteen years later in 1602. His three sons and three daughters are represented on her memorial tablet on opposite sides of a prie-dieu with her father's Coat of Arms and an inscription in Latin[8]. This is complemented by the adjacent 19th century brass plaque which states 'The adjoining monument erected to the pious and beloved memory of the Lady Margaret Poulett who was interred in this Chancel A.D.1602, daughter and heir of Anthony Harvey Esq. and widow of the celebrated Sir Amias Poulett, Knight, Ambassador from Queen Elizabeth to France,

Figure 26. Commemorative plaque for the Peverell family - North Wall of the Nave   (Di Cowan)

and principal keeper to Mary Queen of Scots during her captivity in England, was restored by her descendant The Rt. Hon. Giles 5th Earl Poulett, Viscount Hinton and Baron Poulett of Hinton St. George, Somersetshire in whose family the ancient Manor and Church of Sampford Peverell remained vested from the days of Henry VIIIth to the 55th year of the reign of King George IIIrd.' Apart from one further marble monument, to Margaret Collins who died in 1655, the remaining plaques are 19th century of which the best is that of Elizabeth Dawbney (1809). Of more recent introduction is the War Memorial above the North Door that commemorates those villagers who lost their lives in two World Wars.

On the ground floor of the Tower there are five large painted boards. On the north and south walls are two 'Prayer Boards' with the Ten Commandments and Apostles' Creed: they are dated 1820 and could well have come from the Old Rectory when it ceased to be used as the village school in 1874. On the east wall on the left is the

Figure 27. George I Coat of Arms - 1722 - Tower east wall   *(Di Cowan)*

Royal Coat of Arms of George I dated 1722 (Fig. 27). This was made during the period of the Jacobite rebellions when the inhabitants of the time may have felt it necessary to have a tangible sign of their allegiance to the Crown. In the following year, 1723, all citizens were required to swear the Oath of Allegiance, Supremacy and Abjuration which 83 of the inhabitants of Sampford Peverell duly did (no doubt being those who had more to lose by not doing so). Also on the east wall are two large boards, dated 1750, which contain details of the Sampford Peverell Charity Lands, these boards having been re-painted in 1891. It seems likely that it was formerly on display in the original 'Church House', being the place where the trustees of the Charity Lands had to give account, once a year, of how the rents from these lands had been distributed amongst the poor of the parish. However, the location of the original Church House was forgotten with the passing of time so that in *'The Inquiry into Charity Lands, 1910'* it was said to be 'not now identifiable'.

Churchyard, Gate and Wall

The main entrance to the Churchyard is through a gateway in the western wall (Fig. 28). It is in typical Victorian Gothic style of grey limestone with Hamstone details. A tall double-centred arch with moulded surround is recessed below a chamfered segmental pointed relieving arch. Identical plaques are mounted centrally on either side with the date 1862 though the western facing plaque is too weather-worn to read. The original wrought-iron gates are still in place. The tall stone wall of local red sandstone is much earlier, though the softness of this material has resulted in oft-repeated repair making its origins hard to quantify. Originally there were two entrances to the Church; one from the north along a sunken walled path from Boobery, which is now partially filled in and abandoned, and the other from the south through the wall in the front garden of the Old Rectory. This entrance was installed by Margaret Beaufort to provide a direct access to the Church from the house, but was closed off probably in the early 1800s.

It will be immediately apparent that Sampford Peverell has an unusually small Churchyard. Denis Cluett's *'A Village Childhood'*[9] about his life in Sampford Peverell before the Great War, records that 'the Churchyard extended around three sides of the Church. The fourth side, on the north, was unconsecrated ground and it was here that suicides

Figure 28. Gateway to the Church in the western wall   *(Di Cowan)*

and unbaptised children were buried without the benefit of a funeral service. Unbaptised children were buried here by the father after dark. The village stocks stood against the north side of the church but I never met anyone who could remember their (sic) having been used.' A plan of the 'Manor of Sampford Peverell in the County of Devon the property of the Right Hon. Earl Poulett', surveyed by J. Charlton in 1796, shows that the Church, with its very restricted Churchyard, was surrounded by other village properties and had nowhere to expand. However it is interesting to note that on the consecrated ground to the east, south and west of the Church the land has been built up. Perhaps this was a temporary solution, known to be used by some churches with restricted burial grounds, to provide space for further burials on top of existing graves. This would also serve to explain why the entrance to the Churchyard from the 'Old Rectory' had to be closed as the wall would have had to be rebuilt to contain the weight of earth against it. Nevertheless, by 1880 the Churchyard was virtually full and in 1883 Rossiter Ireland offered a new burial place in Tiverton Road; presumably part of the Rectory garden, which was the priest's property. However, there was an objection from a neighbour, and perhaps for this reason the offer was not followed through.

In 1885, Rossiter Ireland proposed that the rear garden of the then-redundant Old School (formerly the Old Rectory) be used as the new burial ground if he could agree a way of doing so with the Charity Commissioners (the Old School coming under their protection). Under this scheme, the Parish would pay for the new burial ground and a surveyor would be appointed to assess the value of the land. This was accepted by both the Commissioners and the Parish. Later in that same year the trustees, with the support of the Charity Commissioners, agreed to sell the Old School to Rossiter Ireland for £40 and he agreed to convey its back garden to the Parish for the assessed sum of £11.5s0d. He, therefore, became the owner of the Old Rectory, with its reduced garden, which he then rented out.

It is interesting to note that in 1907 Rossiter Ireland recorded, with some bitterness, that the £11.5s0d was never paid to him by the Parish. It seems that all the Parish actually paid for was the construction of the wall behind what is now the Old Rectory, by levying a 4d rate. Rossiter Ireland had paid for the laying out of the ground, the consecration fee and even the entertainment of the Bishop all at his own expense! This extension to the Churchyard served the Parish until the 1950s, when it was formally declared 'closed', although ashes, with small flat tablets, are now accepted for burial. All full interments are carried out in the new Burial Ground on the Tiverton road on the outskirts of the village which was purchased for the Parish in 1926 in memory of a parishioner for £80, together with a Registry Fee of £10.19s 0d.

Today funerals are the preserve of professional members of the Association of Funeral Directors but in earlier times they were the responsibility of the Churchwardens and their Sexton. The Parish had its own bier, a two or four-wheeled trolley with a black oak frame with handles to enable four strong men from the village to transfer the coffin from the deceased's residence to the Church and in latter years from there to the new Burial Ground. The bier was remembered by Cluett as 'a wonderful bit of coachwork that resided in the Coach-house under the stairs leading up to what had been the coachman's quarters' (in the new Rectory, now Church House). These biers were inevitably subject to heavy wear on the rough roads and were regularly replaced. The last 'Parish Bier' was supplied to the Churchwardens in June 1926 by C. Hussey, wheelwright of Moorend, Sampford Peverell for £34; it was recently sold to a Tiverton Funeral Director for restoration.

1.   Church records indicate that the transition from the Saxon *Sanforde* to the English *Sampford Peverell* occurred between 1260 and 1318. Beatrix Cresswell's *Notes on Devon Churches* written in 1920 states 'at the taxation of 1288 *Ecclesia de Sampforde* was included in the Deanery of Tiverton and was valued at 64 shillings and 10 pence'. By 1318 the Lord of the Manor's name Peverell had been added as a suffix and the 'e' of Sampforde was lost over the succeeding century.

2.   Although commonly referred to as Pevsner, *The Buildings of England* second edition published by Penguin in 1989, was written by Bridget Cherry. It was based on the two Devon volumes published by Nicholas Pevsner in 1952. Unless stated elsewhere in the notes all architectural descriptions in quotes are from this source.

3.   Made with a dark igneous stone that extends for the full length of the building and provides a sharp contrast to the lime-washed, now painted, plaster that covers the Sandstone walls.

4.   Cresswell has been quoted here but opinion is divided on the purpose of both these 14th Century recesses. One theory is that the double headed niche on the south side, as illustrated in Figure 14, is the remains of an Easter Sepulchre. A 'piscina', a perforated basin for carrying away the residue of the ablutions, is traditionally sited on the south side of the Altar and this is the author's preferred interpretation. An 'Aumbry' or Ambry is a cupboard for sacramental vessels, which can be placed anywhere within the Sanctuary. The double niche on the north side (Fig. 29) has the necessary recessed stonework but there is no evidence of hinge remains for cupboard doors and its purpose remains uncertain. The Church was provided with an Aumbry in the 15th century wall of the South Aisle (Fig. 30) but all traces of any original fittings were removed when a new door was fitted as part of the creation of the Lady Chapel in 1984.

5.   Tristram Risdon's *Survey of Devon* p.70 re-published by Porcupine, Barnstaple 1970. The remains of this stained glass window were lost when replaced by the Victorian and Edwardian glass that now decorates this part of the Church. The Latin inscription can be translated as 'Mother of the King and wife of Thomas Earl of Derby the said Margaret'.

6.   *Baptismal Fonts of Devon* Devon Archaeological Society 1918 p.583.

7.   Tristram Risdon's *Survey of Devon* p70. It will be immediately apparent that these arms (Fig. 31) are not the same as those illustrated in the Reverend Rossiter Ireland's plaque (see figure 26). Risdon was published in 1811 and thus would have been available to the Rector if he had wanted to be sure that he had included the right Coat of Arms for Sir Hugh Peverell and his family.

8.   The Latin inscription has been translated by the Very Reverend Richard Eyre, sometime Dean of Exeter, as: At the death of the most pious exalted Lady Margaret Powlett, wife of Lord Amias Powlett, Knight of the Garter, I Margaret, whilst it was given me to survive, was happy in my offspring, happy as a parent and as wife to my husband so that all things which concerned me were able to bring me blessing: husband, offspring, an exalted lineage, comeliness, foundation, wealth, a house with a flock of servants, given to hospitality to the needy, a lofty mind and generous hands. Endowed with these good things I lived beloved of people and God and whatever lot the fates gave I bore. Now in death I have returned my soul to the one Lord whom I have served and my lifeless body lies in this sepulchre.

9.   These reminiscences will be published by the Sampford Peverell Society as a separate publication.

*Figure 29. Double headed niche in Sanctuary north wall
(Di Cowan)*

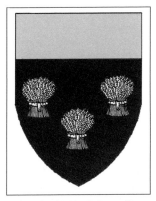

*Figure 30. Aumbry in South
Aisle Lady Chapel   (Di Cowan)*

*Figure 31. Sir Hugh Peverell
Coat of Arms   (Peter Bowers)*

THE CHAPELS*

The Parish Church of St John the Baptist was the established church in the Diocese, but from the end of the 17th century, when severe economic and social changes followed a downturn in the cloth trade, Nonconformity began to have an influence on the life of the village. Commonly referred to at that time as 'Dissenters' these Protestant groups of Baptists, Presbyterians, Independents and Quakers were challenging some disciplines and rites of the Anglican Church with which they did not wish to be associated. In 1662 the Act of Uniformity had made all Nonconformist groups subject to harsh measures, depriving them of the freedom of worship, and driving many of their members to emigrate. In 1689 the Toleration Act gave some relief, but it would be over a century before Nonconformists were allowed to hold political office.

By the beginning of the 18th century, if not before, dissenters from Sampford Peverell were travelling to the neighbouring villages of Uffculme or Halberton where Presbyterian meetings were held. The baptisms and admissions to communion of some of these Sampford residents were recorded by Samuel Short, minister at Uffculme, in the diary he kept from 1705-1726. The number of dissenters varied greatly for according to a report made by Dr John Evans in 1715, almost one in five persons was a dissenter but by 1741 the incumbent at Sampford Peverell, in reply to the visitation queries of the Bishop of Exeter, wrote that of 150 families in the Parish only three were dissenters, of Presbyterian denomination. Nevertheless Nonconformity remained strong in Devon, the Tiverton area being particularly influential[1] and later in the century, although the use of meeting houses declined, chapels were built in their place.

In the 18th century John Wesley founded an evangelical Methodist movement within the Church of England, which became a separate movement in 1795. As well as these Wesleyan Methodists other smaller Methodist groups emerged, later becoming united in the 20th century. Two chapels known to have been established during this time are still to be found in the village. The Wesleyan Methodist Chapel in Higher Town is the oldest Methodist chapel still in use in Devon, having been established in 1802. The other, now privately owned, is a tiny chapel situated further up Higher Town on the opposite side of the road. Believed to have been built by the Baptists around 1800, it later became a place of worship for the Bible Christians, a small Methodist group founded in 1815.

The Wesleyan Methodists

As dissent in its original form became less popular, the new Methodism under its various charismatic leaders became more attractive. Wesleyan Methodism had already come into the area when John Wesley made the first of many visits to Devon in 1739, to comfort his sister-in-law after the death of his brother Samuel, the headmaster of Blundell's School, Tiverton. On many of these visits he must have travelled through Sampford Peverell and on to Halberton where he preached a total of five times. Sadly, he fails to mention Sampford in his Journal though he records visits to other local towns and villages.[2] His final visit to Devon was in 1789, two years before his death, and the last place where he preached was at Halberton. It is said that throughout those 50 years his followers in Sampford would leave their work to look out for him on his journeys through the village.

To gain the protection of the law against 'disturbances' Methodists and other religious groups needed to apply for a licence to regularise their Meeting Houses, which were usually simply a room in a member's house. These licences were issued, on application and payment of a fee, initially by the Bishop's Registrar and subsequently also by the civil Quarter Sessions. There are records[3] of 11 surviving licences granted for Sampford,[4] though the actual number of members remained small. The first of these licences, an application by the Wesleyan Methodists, was granted on 9th December 1793 for Samuel Jennings' kitchen, and 10 days later on 19th December, for Robert Webber's kitchen. In November 1800 Francis Taylor's former kitchen was called into service but on 1st October 1802 the first licence was granted for the 'newly erected house belonging to trustees', the present Wesleyan Chapel (Fig. 32).

No records survive to explain how it was possible for a struggling Methodist cause in the early 19th century, meeting in Francis Taylor's converted kitchen with a membership of only 13, to achieve the building of a new purpose-built chapel with

Figure 32. The Wesleyan Chapel viewed from Higher Town road   *(Di Cowan)*

room for many more. From surviving Circuit accounts, which begin at Christmas 1777, it appears that the Sampford members contributed 13 shillings a quarter, about £32 today. This money, attributed 'to a friend', was paid fairly regularly until 1796, when it became acknowledged as from 'a friend from Sampford': thereafter Sampford Peverell paid its own contribution of 13 shillings each quarter until 1801. These accounts provide the earliest confirmation of a Methodist cause in the village, with seven members in 1777 rising within six months to 19, but which by 1801 had declined to just four. Yet, despite this weakness in Methodist support, money was regularly sent to the circuit and capital was provided to build their new chapel. Roger Thorne suggests that there must have been a local benefactor; this has been supported by the researches undertaken by the late Alan Voce of Tiverton Museum.[5] In 1993, when looking through some miscellaneous papers in the Circuit safe, he found a letter written from London on 29th May 1803 by a Mr Samuel Jennings to Mr W. Hellyer of Sampford Peverell. Here, Samuel Jennings states that he has paid for the new building and is anxious and annoyed that he has had no news of its progress. From the evidence of the licence dated 1st October 1802[6], it appears that the Chapel was already up and running, complete with a Minister, Joseph Algar, and a Board of Trustees (see Appendix 4). The Board, presumably unknown to Mr Jennings the benefactor, included two gentlemen with the name William Hellyer and another Samuel Jennings! 'Long has my patience been tried', his letter begins, but without saying how long that was. 'Some considerable time since' he had sent off twenty pounds to Mr Cowlen[7], which was 'more than enough to finish the chappell', but has heard nothing and he asks for Hellyer's niece to send a report about the Chapel and Mr Cowlen 'without disguise'. It may have been that the building was in use though not finished and nobody thought to tell him! Samuel Jennings gives the motives for his benevolence to the fact that his father is a Methodist (possibly the Samuel Jennings given as one of the original Trustees) and that he himself is sympathetic to the cause. He also states that he is aware that the previous place of worship (Francis Taylor's former kitchen) is in a ruinous condition and ill-befits its purpose. It seems likely that he continued to support the Chapel as the records show that a Samuel Jennings from Rotherhithe, Surrey, is included in the list of Trustees in 1820.[8]

Throughout the 19th century worship at Sampford Peverell was very much the same as other Methodist chapels in the circuit. Many of Wesley's followers would attend their Parish Church in the normal way and meet in the afternoon or evening to sing Wesley's hymns and discuss their particular views. Their singing was probably accompanied by a couple of stringed instruments rather than an organ, and collections were intermittent as some members would have been too poor to contribute every week. The oldest known circuit plan is from April to October 1825, when Sampford had services at 2 pm and 6 pm. In that quarter the sacrament was administered twice. Twenty-five years later the plan from February to May shows services at 10.30 am and 6 pm, with week-night preaching on Wednesdays at

Figure 33. The Wesleyan Chapel viewed from Sampford Barton lane   *(Di Cowan)*

Figure 34. The Wesleyan Chapel and New Inn - circa 1950

7 pm. In the 1850 plan there was one communion and one love-feast,[9] both in the evening, and small print draws attention to special events on many Sundays, including an address to the Sunday School children and the monthly Missionary Prayer meeting. There were collections for the Circuit Debt, the Chapel and Education Fund, Worn-out Ministers, the Local Preachers Fund as well as the Quarterly Collection. For the first half of the 20th century, as numbers increased, the choir and Sunday School sat in the gallery, which they shared with the organ. In the 1950s Sunday School attendance rose to 50 and outings were introduced, which became an occasion for the whole village, with coaches going to Weymouth, Paignton or Bristol Zoo. In recent years membership has declined again but in 2003 the Chapel congregation was joined by the Anglicans in celebration of 200 years of Methodist worship in Sampford Peverell.

Building the Chapel

The Chapel was built on what was originally a garden plot. It was not the most suitable site (Fig. 33), but it became available and was bought by the Methodists, presumably with their benefactor's money. Before 1802 the present western half of the site was fenced off and occupied by two cottages opposite the New Inn, now a private house (Fig. 34). On the eastern part of the site there was a cottage known as Candy's house and the rest was garden sandwiched between the road to the Barton and Fore Street (now Higher Town). Candy's house came on to the market in 1819; it was sold to the Trustees for £36 and pulled down to open up the eastern

Figure 35. 'Marble Arch' cottages at the top of the lane from Higher Town to The Barton - circa 1915

end of the site. Twenty-four years later the land at the western end came on the market for £50. In 1844 this was duly conveyed to the Methodists and the cottages were demolished to provide the graveyard that can be seen today. The present grassed area between the steps beside the Chapel gate on the east side and the lane was formerly occupied by three picturesque old cottages, one of which spanned the road to the mill and the Barton with an arch; sadly all were destroyed in a house fire in 1938 (Fig. 35).

The Wesleyan Chapel is a plain rendered structure built on a steeply sloping site between the two lanes, which lead down from Higher Town to Sampford Barton Farm and the former mill. It is perched on the side of the valley to the north of the village with a view that now looks across to the North Devon Link road and the site of the former castle. Below the Chapel there was a large mill pond known as 'Great Pond',which, until it was drained in the 1930s, was a striking feature of the village. It can be seen on the early maps and old photographs to the west of Barton Farm (Fig. 36). The north wall of the Chapel rests on a massive brick and masonry retaining wall that forms the boundary of the site. The property now consists of the Chapel, with a porch on its eastern side, and the Sunday school and kitchen, which was built on to the west end of the building. It is unfortunate that although it is only 200 years since the Chapel was built, there is little documentary evidence of its construction; its history is limited to the Tithe Map of 1844 and the building itself.

Figure 36. View of Sampford Barton and the Great Pond from near the Chapel - circa 1920

Figure 37. Chapel interior *(Di Cowan)*

Roger Thorne describes the Chapel as having a 'rendered and pedimented open porch, with the date 1803, giving access to a narrow vestibule, at each end of which are stairs to the gallery. The gallery is less than 10 feet deep and its front is supported on thin wooden columns. Doors from the vestibule open to the interior, giving access to the two aisles between the pews (Fig.37). At the front is a small rostrum pulpit below a classical wooden tablet with the text "We preach not ourselves but Christ Jesus as Lord"[10] (Fig. 38), which comes from the Revised Version that was issued in 1881. 'In the east wall there are two round-headed windows above the porch and gallery and low down in the south wall there are three segmental-headed windows. The north wall has three windows, two of which match those in the south wall but one is round-headed

Figure 38. Rostrum and Tablet *(Di Cowan)*

Figure 39. Chapel Gallery   *(Di Cowan)*

and set higher to light (Fig. 39) the end of the gallery. High up in the west wall of the original Chapel are two segmental-headed windows, which now look into the upper floor of the Sunday School. There is no evidence under the floor at the east end to suggest that the Chapel has been lengthened there but the arrangement of the windows suggests that the walls have been raised: this was probably done when the gallery and rear vestibule were inserted in the 1840s when the membership was high. Higher windows with rounded heads were built into the east end to clear the gallery and one of the north wall windows raised to give it light. The windows above the pulpit appear high but have segmental heads so may be original.'

'The sole surviving account book of the Chapel Trust is generally uninformative but in early 1871 refers to whitewashing and colouring, including the school. This is the first reference to the school and suggests that it was not new at that date. In 1872 the accounts mention the cost of work by masons, joiners and painters for restoring and reseating the chapel and for lamps and fittings, particularly at the porch and chapel entrance. This came to £118 15s but descriptions like "restoration" can be very difficult to define in terms of what was actually done'. In the early days from 1802 seating would have been on benches, with men and women sitting on opposite sides of the Chapel, but by the time of this restoration the forms had been replaced with wooden pews arranged at the sides and down the centre of the Chapel. An article in the Tiverton Gazette dated 6th August 1872[11] headed "Wesleyan Chapel Re-Opening" described the services on the preceding Thursday, August 1st. In the afternoon the Rev. V. Cowell Brown of Exeter preached on "What are these which are arrayed in white robes ..." the room having been "tastefully decorated for the occasion" and then everybody adjourned to the schoolroom, where 100 sat down to tea. In the evening the healthy financial situation was described by Richard Jennings and there were "good and stirring addresses" by two ministers and three laymen.'[12] The article continues, "Thanks were given to the Messrs. Jennings, who had so energetically exerted themselves for the accomplishment of that laudable undertaking - the renovation of the chapel". The preaching continued the following Sunday, "listened to by attentive congregations. Miss Jennings presided at the harmonium." The newspaper report had described the Chapel as a "neat little edifice ...but sufficiently large

Figure 40. Wesleyan Chapel exterior before rendering - circa 1890

for the present wants of the inhabitants", which clearly irritated the members. In the following week there is an indignant letter from Richard Jennings, the steward, who insisted that 'the words "neat little edifice" may mislead some of our friends who live at a distance. You will oblige me by inserting in your next issue the subjoined internal dimensions of the Chapel and Sunday Schoolroom, making together with the yard in which the buildings stand a valuable freehold connexional property; Chapel 36ft x 26ft and 21ft high, Sunday Schoolroom, 26ft x 18ft and 21ft high'.[13] (Fig. 40)

Roger Thorne notes that 'the two-storey Sunday School is built on to the west end of the Chapel, with internal access from doorways either side of the pulpit. Stairs in the south east corner lead to the upper floor. At some time this was partitioned to serve as a caretaker's flat and the partitions survived until recent years.' No records survive to provide an accurate date for the Sunday School extension except to place it between 1844 and 1870; the architectural style would indicate a date nearer the latter. It also seems likely that the upper floor was later, being inserted after the school extension had been completed.

'The three walls of the school are rough masonry, probably local stone. The fourth wall, which is the end of the Chapel and appears to be brick, has a skin of masonry built against its face to support the floor joists. The south end of this wall is built on a massive block of Sampford sandstone and there is a horizontal reef of the same stone projecting out under the school, both of which appear to be bed-rock but with a suggestion of excavation. Seen from the lower road, the Chapel looks something of an eyrie, as the retaining wall is about 12 feet high.' The Tithe Map of 1844 describes the site as 'Chapel and Yard'. 'In the 1860s and later the Chapel account-book refers to "cleaning the yard", suggesting a surfaced area but today no trace remains.'

There are graves to the east and west of the Chapel but the graveyard is very steep and limited in space. At the back there are around a dozen gravestones and at the front there are six more, but it is probable that all available room is filled with interments. Some older Chapel members can remember graves being blasted out of the underlying rock by local quarrymen. Most of the older gravestones are worn and difficult to decipher but near the porch on the right-hand side is the grave of Eliza Osborn, the wife of the Reverend John Osborn, who had been appointed as the Superintendent Minister of the circuit for the year 1848-1849.[14] She died six months later on the 8th March 1850.

The Other Nonconformists in Sampford Peverell

Baptists

While the Wesleyan Methodists were consolidating their membership in Sampford Peverell in the late 18th century, the Baptists were also meeting in local houses. Licences were obtained in July 1799 for John Hellier's house and in 1805 for Catherine Webber's house. Then, in May 1806, they purchased or built a permanent meeting place - 'a house called the Baptist Chapel in the town'.

It is an interesting reflection of the times that while two groups of Nonconformists in the village had acquired new chapels in the early 19th century the Parish Church was in dire need of restoration! In 1821 the Bishop of Exeter had asked his clergy for details of their parishes,[15] and in reply the Rector Simon Pidsley complained that Sampford Peverell Church was dilapidated and not safe to be used. The canal company had pulled down part of his Rectory and built the canal through his garden but they had not got round to building his new Rectory. About the local Nonconformists he was remarkably uninformative, 'There are no Papists, but Methodists, and a few Anabaptists - I have no means of knowing whether they are licensed or not.' From this correspondence it is clear that in 1821 the presence of practising Baptists in Sampford Peverell was known to both the Rector and his Bishop. However, it must be assumed that their membership was in decline for there is no reference to Sampford Peverell in the national list of Baptist Chapels in 1827.[16] Whether this Chapel remained in use between 1822 and 1850 is uncertain, but its future lay with the Bible Christians.

The Bible Christians

In 1815 the Bible Christians, the smallest of the Methodist denominations, came into being, their followers mainly coming from North Cornwall, North Devon and West Somerset. They became known as 'Bryonites' after their founder William O'Brian.[17] O'Brian was later succeeded by the Thorne family from Shebbear in North Devon where the headquarters of the denomination remained for some years. They were strongest in the rural and fishing communities of the South West peninsula, meeting in the open, in cottages, and later in their own chapels. By 1822 this new Methodist group had become established in the Tiverton area. In 1832 they were licensed to meet in John Goffin's house in Sampford Peverell. Bible Christian records show that in 1842 their actual membership was tiny, with only four committed members, but within three years the local minister was proposing to preach at services at Halberton and Sampford twice every Sunday! According to Mrs Joan Wright, a former long-term resident of Sampford Peverell, her great-grandmother, Mrs Elizabeth Saunders (née Dyke) born 1822, would take a turn once a month to preach for the Bible Christians. This remarkable woman, aged 18, would rise at

Figure 41. Former Bible Christian or 'Bryonite' Chapel in Higher Town　　　　　*(Di Cowan)*

4am and walk eight miles from her family home in Rackenford into Tiverton to preach the morning service. After dinner she resumed her journey towards Halberton to take afternoon service there and then tramped on to Sampford Peverell for the evening service. There she slept the night, returning home the next day. Elizabeth later set up a millinery business in Sampford and at the age of 23 married a local mason, Luke Saunders. They were married for over 40 years and had seven children. When the Bible Christians ceased holding services at Sampford she joined the Wesleyan Methodists. Mrs Saunders died in 1926, just 8 days short of her 104th birthday. Her 100th birthday and her obituary were the subject of articles in local newspapers.

Around the mid 19th century the Sampford Peverell Bible Christians felt strong enough to consider renting or borrowing the disused Baptist Chapel. On the tithe map of 1844 the Chapel is shown as 'Bryonite Chapel and Waste', in the ownership of William Wood and occupied by himself, so it would appear to have been in use by the Bible Christians then (Fig. 41). In 1850 the circuit bought the Chapel from the Uffculme Baptists for £12 and received their licence on 4th October 1851. Membership still hovered around single figures and the Chapel actually closed for two years. During the following ten years membership increased, at times reaching double figures in the early 1860s, but then tailed off again so that by 1870 it was resolved to sell the Chapel by tender.

'A note in the circuit records says it was 21 feet by 13 feet by 12 feet high - internal measurements that correspond with the building that survives on the south side of what was then called Fore Street, now known as Higher Town, 80 yards west of the Methodist chapel. On the road side is a single arched lancet window and on the house side are two arched doorways. It is almost certain that in 1806 the windows would have been built with square-heads and that the conversion to arched tops was undertaken by the Bible Christians, probably in the 1860s. There is virtually no indication inside of its former use as a chapel although it is likely that the pulpit was at the west end. The east end was blank until its recent conversion to a garage, so it is possible that one of the two arched doors is original and the other is a window cut down. Until recently it was divided by a partition which explains the two doors.'

* The writer of this chapter is indebted to the work and research of Roger Thorne in his definitive work on the Sampford Methodists, *'History and Mystery in Sampford Peverell'* 1993. Extensive use has been made of this work, indicated in this chapter by inverted commas.

1   The Uffculme Meeting later became Congregational; the Halberton one closed in 1780.
2   Tiverton, Cullompton, Uffculme, Maiden Down, Halberton, Bampton and Culmstock, see M. Wickes: *John Wesley in Devon* pp 13-17.
3   Devon Record Office - Meeting House Licences at the Bishop's Registry.
4   See Appendix 1.
5   Following his retirement in 1984 Alan Voce [1928-2006] served at various times in an honorary capacity as Curator, Secretary, Chairman and genealogist at Tiverton Museum until his death. He was a lifelong Methodist.

6   *A Chronological history of people called Methodists:* Myles, W. The 1813 edition gives the date of the chapel as 1802.

7   A Mr John Cowlen appears in the list of Trustees for 1820. See Appendix 3.

8   The Parish registers record baptisms of the children of a Samuel and Elizabeth Jennings, including Richard 1767, Samuel 1768 and Joseph 1772. Joseph and his wife Mary had a son Richard born 1810 who may have been the Richard Jennings who wrote the letter to the Tiverton Gazette in 1872, referred to later. There is no record of Samuel (1768) having married or had children baptised in the Parish so possibly he is the Samuel Jennings of Surrey having moved away. Certainly it seems that the Jennings family were very involved in the chapel for many years.

9   Love-feast or agape - a feast in celebration of selfless Christian love, modelled on that held by the early Christians at communion time, when gifts were given for the poor.

10   II Cor.iv.5 Revised Version.

11   *Tiverton Gazette and East Devon Herald* 6th August 1872.

12   Ibid - Revs. W. Cowell-Brown of Exeter and J. Edwards, Tiverton, Mssrs. Minninet of Westleigh, W.C. Bennett of Tiverton and Stadling of Culmstock.

13   *Tiverton Gazette and East Devon Herald* 13th August 1872.

14   *Hall's Circuits and Ministers 1765-1912:* Joseph Hall.

15   The Diocese of Exeter in 1821: Bishop Carey's replies to queries before visitation: M. Cook.

16   Two early 19th century lists of Baptist churches from the Baptist Magazine 1990.

17   In 1831 William O'Brian became estranged from the movement he founded and left with his wife for America where he travelled as an itinerant preacher in the US and Canada, and later died there.

Figure 42. The Old Rectory as it is today

(Di Cowan)

THE RECTORIES

Inextricably woven with the history of the Church is that of the properties that were provided as residences for Parish Priests. In the early mediaeval period accommodation might have been available in the Castle but usually the priest was given a small house within the village near his Church. Later, houses were much larger and served several purposes. To summarise R.J. Brown in his *Extracts from English Village Architecture,* the mediaeval church not only served the village community for religious worship, but was also the focus of social life in the village, holding feasts and festivals, in the usually pew-less church, which were effective in supplementing church funds and supporting the poorer village families. In the early 16th century such frivolity, including the sale of wine and beer, was frowned upon in the church and 'church houses' were commonly built close to the church acting as a predecessor for the village hall. These houses were generally two storey, often of ashlar, with an outside spiral staircase leading to a single upper room.[1]

In Sampford Peverell nothing is known of any church dwellings or 'houses' before 1500, but it seems probable that there would have been an old, perhaps thatched, cob cottage, followed by a stone hall, for the mediaeval priests within easy reach of the church. The oldest surviving Rectory was built by Margaret, Countess of Richmond and Derby, in 1500. She had inherited the Manor from her grandfather John Beaufort, Earl of Somerset, in about 1480 and is believed to have spent some time in the village, probably residing in Sampford Castle (now demolished) whilst her son Henry Tudor was fighting for the English throne. Between 1495 and 1500 she provided sufficient funds to add a South Aisle and Porch to the church and to build a house (the 'Old Rectory') in the field to the south of the church. Whether conceived as a 'Rectorye', as it is described in the earliest terriers, 'church house' or school, successive rectors used this residence as their home for over three centuries (Fig. 42).

In 1811 the Grand Western Canal Company started building the canal, which was planned to run from Taunton to Topsham with a branch to Tiverton that passed through Sampford Peverell. The course of this canal through the village required part of the Old Rectory to be knocked down and the loss of a considerable amount of its land. In compensation the Canal Company was required to build a new Rectory but, although the canal was completed in 1813, it was not until 1841 that sufficient funds were available and the Rectory, now 'Church House', was handed over to the parish. Extracts from *'The Inquiry into Charity Lands, 1910'* show that the Old Rectory was taken over by the Canal Company and in 1844 granted to a body of Trustees, chaired by the then Rector Dr Boulton, to be used as a National School for the 'education of labouring, manufacturing and other poorer classes in the parish'.[2] Records indicate that Richmond House, as it was then known, continued in this role throughout the 1850s and 1860s, at one point having 75 scholars, until the Reverend Rossiter Ireland provided Sampford Peverell with a new school in 1874. The Trustees, with the approval of the Charity Commission, sold the property to the Reverend Rossiter Ireland in 1885. On his death in 1908 the property was given to his niece Mary. She was married to Philip Rossiter, Rector for two years until his death in 1910, and she continued to live in the house until her death in 1957.

The new Rectory (Church House) served the parish as home for their Rectors and as a meeting place for the Parochial Church Council for a hundred and fifty years. Around 1990, at a time when Church of England funds were severely pressed, this house was assessed as too expensive to maintain, being in need of major repair and modernisation. The decision was made to sell the Rectory and most of its garden to realise sufficient funds to build a New Rectory on the small remaining plot of parish land. This Rectory remains to serve the parish, now part of the Sampford Peverell Team Ministry, into the 21st century.

The Old Rectory (Grade 2* listed)

The Old Rectory was built in the late 15th century and is constructed of local Sampford stone, a coarse red sandstone from quarries to the north of the village. It is typically Tudor in style, but is L-shaped, comprising only one solar wing on the left (northern) side. The house faces west and is entered through a large Tudor double door of oak with a flattened, four centred, moulded arch. Above the door a plaque reads 'Margaret [Countess of] Richmond, Derby. House and School of St John the Baptist. Erected A.D. 1500. Restored 1850. Prepare ye the way of the Lord. Make his paths straight'.(Fig. 43) On the left of a small passageway (originally the screens-passage) is the main hall, now the dining room, with an impressive fireplace against the front wall, between two windows, which are now modernised. The chimneystack is a significant feature of the front of the house, and only the upper part appears to have been renovated. The hall leads to the main reception room in the solar wing running from the front to the rear of the property, with windows on the west and eastern sides, and a fireplace on the northern wall. Both of these rooms have impressive original oak-boxed ceilings (Fig. 44). The reception room, or parlour as it was, is unusual in having two external doors. It is known that this room was later used as a school; it is possible

Figure 43. Old Rectory Tudor Door and commemorative tablet   *(Di Cowan)*

48

that the arched door on the south-western side of the solar wing, which leads out into the front drive, was built to allow for a separate entrance.

Above the reception room the solar has an ornately carved barrel-vaulted ceiling with eight bays. It is now divided into three rooms and a passageway, but one original cross-partition near the east end must have divided the wing into a small eastern room of about two bays, perhaps an ante room, and a larger room of six bays, which would have provided sleeping quarters and private living areas for the priest and his family. This room has a fireplace and several windows (one blocked) and includes a small, original slit in the south wall overlooking the entrance. Nothing remains of any original stairway to this upper floor, but this was probably accessed by an oak staircase removed in the late 1840s. There is also the possibility that an outside spiral

Figure 44. The Old Rectory oak-boxed ceiling (Di Cowan)

staircase existed on the east side between the hall and parlour but there is no evidence remaining to substantiate this theory.

To the right of the front door and passage are the kitchen and utility rooms, which may well have been the original buttery and pantry. A small two-storey annex, referred to as the 'south wing' was attached to the south-east corner of the house in the 17th century but, at the time of the construction of the canal, this was removed.

The central hall of the house was, like the Solar wing, built with two storeys. During the incumbency of Dr Anthony Boulton (1847-54) the upper level of the hall, together with its fine oak staircase, was removed by the Trustees of the property. It can only be assumed that the roof was rotten or riddled with worm for such a drastic solution to have been taken and this action was severely criticised by Rossiter Ireland. A photograph taken in 1890 shows Mr Bowden, the tenant of the Reverend Rossiter Ireland and his Church Warden, with his wife in the front garden of the Old Rectory or Richmond House as it was known at the time. Behind them, in this unique picture, the middle of the house can be seen to have only one storey (Fig. 45). The upper storey was replaced in 1912 by Mary Rossiter, following the death of her husband, to provide additional bedrooms. At the same time she extended the central portion of the house to the rear (east) to provide the replacement staircase and a lavatory.

Figure 45. Mr and Mrs Bowden, tenants of the Reverend Rossiter Ireland in the Old Rectory in 1890

In the 16th century the land belonging to the Old Rectory was quite extensive. An early, undated, terrier suggests that 'there is belonging unto the Rectorye or Parsonage, a mansion or dwelling howse, with large courtlidge and a garden, contayninge one acre of ground, or neere thereabouts. There are belonging to the Rectorye three closes of land, and one meadow thereunto adjoining, all which premises are called Highe Wood, and contayne seven acres'. An extract from the terriers from 1605 indicates that there were nine tenements 'which have bin with held by the Pouletts from the said Rectorye, sithens the dayes of King Edward the sixth', whose tenants included two widows, a weaver and a tanner. The terrier from 1680 suggests that the Rectory had two barns, one stable and two courts within the acre of land surrounding the house. It mentions glebe lands comprising four closes of land at High Wood, and a further half acre of meadow at Humphry Pullens, and also a burgesse acre in David Yarn's western meadow, called More Lake. 'For justments ye parishioners do pay twenty pence of a pound, and all the rest tythes in kinde, excepting aples, for which they do pay two pence a hogshead for sider and, excepting hay if it be old stock meadow and not let out to a yearly rent, for which they do pay two pence an acre, but if it be let out they do pay twenty pence of a pound, and excepting milk for which they do pay fower pence for a cow and three pence for a heifer. For easter dutyes fower pence for each man and his wife, and two pence for a single person above ye age of sixteen yeares'.

Most of the land and functional buildings to the south and east of the Old Rectory were lost when the canal was built, and almost all the remaining garden at the back of the house was given up by the Reverend Rossiter Ireland and his co-trustees in 1885 to provide additional land for burials as the adjacent churchyard was virtually full. A retaining wall was built close to the rear of the Old Rectory, the cost of which was included in the four-penny rate raised by the parish to pay for the extended Churchyard.

Figure 46. Plaque on Old Rectory garage salvaged from the arched gate *(Di Cowan)*

Today the front of the Old Rectory contains a well laid out garden bounded on the western side from the road by a high wall passing up to the Churchyard. In 1960 the then owner of the property, proud to be one of the first in the village to own a motor car, astonished parishioners by knocking down the beautiful arched gate to the house so that he could get his new motorcar up to his front door! This arched gateway had originally been situated on the north wall of the property, adjoining the Churchyard and providing the Rector with direct access to his Church. It was taken down and moved to the front of the house in the early 18th century when the burial ground was raised and the wall rebuilt. There seems to have been a good deal of adverse comment about the demolition in the local press, which led the offender to salvage the plaque, originally situated on the gate, and to place it within the wall of his new garage. The plaque reads 'Margaret, Countess of Richmond, AD 1500. Learn To Do Well', which, was probably placed there by the then Rector and confirms that the house was used as a school after its renovation (Fig. 46).

The Rectory (Church House) (Grade 2 listed)

The decision to build the Grand Western Canal was conceived in 1769, but the Sampford Peverell section was not undertaken until 1813. The canal cuts through the centre of the village, which required the destruction of a number of houses in the village and much of the grounds and stable buildings, including a portion of the south east wing of the Rectory (Old Rectory). As part of the planning consent the Grand Western Canal Company was obliged to purchase or build another parsonage house within three years as compensation for the loss. However, severe financial difficulties within the company caused a prolonged delay; legal arguments became protracted, and many years passed before the work was undertaken.

A document dated 1820, entitled '*Justification for building a new Parsonage House and Sundry Offices at Sampford Peverell*', goes into great detail about the standard of accommodation required by the Church. The wood throughout the house was to comprise 'oak joists and door lintels, with red or white deal, or Norway Timber (varieties of fir or pine) for floor-boards etc. The walls were to be lath and plaster, except the back kitchen to be rendered. The principal reception room and bedrooms should have $1\frac{3}{4}$ inch 6-panelled doors with sturdy locks, and the other rooms to be ledged doors, with inferior quality fastenings. The principal rooms should have window shutters hung in two heights with boxing, and simple shutters or iron bars to the back kitchen and pantry. A plaster cornice with enrichment in the drawing room, and plain plaster cornice in the dining room and best staircase. Two Devonshire marble chimney pieces with Portland slabs for the principal rooms, stone chimney pieces and slabs for the bedrooms, and stone slabs and wood dressing for the maid's room and kitchen.

Figure 47. The Rectory (Church House) as it is today   *(Catherine McMurty)*

Windows on the south and two side fronts to be lined with glass, but casement windows with leaded glass to the kitchen, pantry and dairy rooms. The foundations are to be dug to provide for the building of cellars (for wine, beer and coal) with an oak staircase leading down, pebble pitching on the floor, and whitewash throughout. All gutters and water shoots to be lead lined. A well should be dug and brick lined, with a lead pump, oak carriages and pump trough. A 52-foot barn should be built with stone walls 20 inches thick, and finished with oak doors and floors and thatched roof. Also a 32-foot wide thatched, stone walled stable and gig house, with an elm manger and two stalls being separated from the gig house by oak partitioning'.

The house, which stands on a small knoll opposite the church occupying the corner plot between Turnpike and Higher Town, was completed in 1841 (Fig. 47). A plaque above the front door shows the coat of arms of the Bishopric of Exeter and reads 'E. Pidsley, Rector, 1841'. The house is a large, square, Victorian style property, with the front entrance porch facing east and the main reception rooms on either side. Although the house is now rendered, evidence that the house was built of red local stone, similar to the Old Rectory, can be seen on an inside wall where the modern garage joins the house. The east and south elevations of the house have French windows from the dining, drawing and sitting rooms leading out onto the garden. Upper windows are smaller and have Tudor style stonework.

From the front door a long hall leads to a large inner square hall containing the main staircase and a cupola ceiling light, octagonal in shape, with stained glass design. The principal downstairs rooms are the drawing and dining rooms, a sitting room, study, office and kitchen/utility area. The main staircase curves up from the hall, with a small secondary staircase branching off to the right half way up. There are eight rooms on the upper floor, originally seven bedrooms and a servant's room. The upstairs rooms used to have small fireplaces, but all have been blocked up or removed over the years. Downstairs fireplaces only remain in the drawing and sitting rooms. These rooms and the dining room still have working shutters and many have original glass and decorative astragals (Fig. 48). A scullery extended the property on the northwest side, close to the site of the old stable and coach house.

Figure 48. The Rectory (Church House) windows (Di Cowan)

In 1841, when the property was handed over to the Reverend Pidsley (1835-1847), a deed map showed that the grounds belonging to the Rectory extended along the turnpike road for some distance. It also indicated that a small corner plot on the bend of Higher Town and Turnpike, within the garden of the Rectory, had contained a separate dwelling, although later maps show this to have disappeared. Documents also show that although the Glebe land of nine acres at High Wood existed in 1880, by 1930 it had all been sold.

During the Second World War many country properties were surveyed for surplus accommodation. By 1942 Tiverton Rural District Council had requisitioned the Rectory for use as a hospital for evacuee children and the Rector, Reverend JG Brunskill (1940-1944), lived in the parish house at Uplowman. Two years later the Council gave it up, but they wanted recompense from the Diocese for installing a boiler and an airing cupboard! The Rector politely implored the Diocese to agree to some remuneration, otherwise he 'will be completely without hot water'. He also requested the installation of a separate downstairs cloakroom, as he 'will soon have imposed upon him six difficult evacuees: the need is for health, not luxury'!

In that same year, 1944, correspondence shows that plans were being drawn up to subdivide the Rectory. Wartime need for rural housing was great, and it was considered too large for the Rector and his family. By 1945 the house had been subdivided to provide a maisonette, comprising the greater part of the upper floor, with stairs leading down into what had been the pantry (now the utility room). The original maid's bedroom and children's nursery bedroom on the north side were converted into a kitchen and bathroom. A partition wall was erected at the back of the staircase on the top floor with a Perspex upper section to allow light through and a dividing door on the short passage to separate the two dwellings. From 1945, the Reverend Coyle, who had been installed as Rector in 1944 , lived with his family in the main part of the house downstairs and had two bedrooms on the upper floor. The rental income from the maisonette supplemented his available funds considerably but within 10 years, the maisonette was no longer let and in 1953 he took over the whole property again.

In 1946 the Diocese were concerned that the stables and coach house, which were by that time in a state of considerable disrepair, required major funding to keep them functional. Two years later there were further problems when dry rot was discovered in the floorboards of some of the lower rooms and the surveyor's report highlighted fungus growing on the walls in the cellars. No repairs appear to have been made at this time to rectify any of these major defects. In the early 1950s further correspondence between the Rector and the Church Commissioners and Diocesan Dilapidations Board highlighted the deep financial struggle faced by Rectors to pay for even minor repairs to the house, outbuildings and grounds from their church income. Grants could be obtained for certain works, but only after months of requests, and when a deficit occurred, funds had to be found from the incumbent's own income, which at times caused great distress and hardship. An electric cooker bought on hire purchase by the Reverend Coyle, who requested some payment support, involved months of correspondence between the Dilapidations Board in Exeter and the Commissioners in Westminster, both trying to avoid any involvement or responsibility.

No distinctive records have so far come to light regarding the major work finally agreed to be carried out to the Rectory, but it is believed that in the early 1960s a

Figure 49. The Rectory (Church House) as constructed with Regency style veranda

local building company, on the verge of bankruptcy after several bad winters, undertook significant alterations to the house, which kept the company afloat. A local newspaper dated July 10th 1964, states that an old chest was discovered by the Reverend Hardy in the back of his garage, the former coach house. This chest with its '6 padlock staples' contained many old, severely damaged documents, chronicling village life, which are now in the possession of the Devon Records Office. During these alterations, the stables and coach house were demolished so that a seven-foot wall on two sides is all that now remains of the stables. The cellars appear to have been completely filled in with the rubble from the demolition of the stables and the removal of all conversions of the maisonette. Concrete floors replaced the rotting original wooden floors on the ground floor level. The scullery was removed and a complete wing added on to the north side, to provide a second kitchen, a boot room or lobby, and a new garage. The well was filled in and the Regency style veranda (Fig. 49), which had covered almost the full length of the south elevation, was also removed. In 1993 the Rectory was sold privately, and from that time has been known as Church House. It has since received modernisation and restoration, but many of the original features of a Victorian parsonage have been retained.

The New Rectory

Towards the end of the 20th century it was clear to the Church Commissioners that large Rectories, such as Church House in Sampford Peverell, were too expensive to maintain. The strip of land belonging to the Rectory along the Turnpike road was separated, with two new houses built here and the properties sold privately. A new Rectory was built on a plot to the west of Church House, which had been part of the land leased to the village school, and in 1992 this became the New Rectory. Although, unlike its two predecessors, the New Rectory is no longer right in the heart of the village (Fig. 50), the house provides the incumbent with a modern, low maintenance and economical dwelling.

Figure 50. The road to Higher Town from Lower Town between the Parish Church and the former Rectories - circa 1970

Notes:

1. Brown R J (2004: 193) *Extracts from English Village Architecture*. Robert Hale, London
2. Sampford Peverell parochial church records - Devon Record Office.

Figure 51. In front of The Rectory: School Choir with Mr T.J. Samuels (headmaster), Reverend J.J. Rees (Rector 1911-1939) and Mrs Samuels, 1938

Figure 52. In The Rectory garden: Church Choir with Reverend J.N. Hardy (Rector 1962-1967), 1964

BIBLIOGRAPHY AND OFFICIAL RECORDS

Bridget Cherry & Nikolaus Pevsner: *The Buildings of England – Devon – second edition (Revised).* Penguin 1989

Michael Cook: *The Diocese of Exeter in 1821; Bishop Carey's replies to queries before visitation.* Devon and Cornwall Record Society 1960

Beatrix Cresswell: *History of Devon Churches.* 1920

Joseph Hall: *Hall's Circuits and Ministers. An alphabetical list of the circuits in Great Britain 1765-1912.* 1913

Helen Harris: *The Grand Western Canal.* David & Charles 1973

Rev. Daniel and Samuel Lysons: *Magna Britannia Vol. VI (Devonshire Part II).* Thomas Cadell, London 1822

W. Myles: *A Chronological History of the people called Methodists.* Third and Fourth Editions dated 1803 and 1813

Tristram Risdon: *The Chorographical Description of Survey of the County of Devon.* (Written 1605 and first published 1811) reprinted by Porcupines Barnstaple 1970

Peter Sainsbury: *The Transition from Tradition to Technology: A History of the Dairy Industry in Devon.* P.T.Sainsbury 1991

Roger Thorne: *History and Mystery in Sampford Peverell.* 1993

Peter Underwood: *Ghosts of Devon.* Bossinney Books 1982

Arthur Warne: *Church and Society in 18th Century Devon.* David & Charles 1969

M. Wickes: *Devon in the Religious Census of 1851.* 1990

M. Wickes (ed): *John Wesley in Devon 1739-1789.* 1985

OFFICIAL RECORDS

Alecto Historical Editions: *The Devonshire Domesday.* Introduction by Frank Barlow 1991

Devon Archaeological Society: *Proceedings*

Devon County Council: *Sundry documents, records, papers and maps.* Devon Record Office

Devon County Council: *Sites and Monuments Register.* County Hall

Sampford Peverell: *Parish Registers.* Tiverton Museum of Mid-Devon Life

Sherborne Mercury

Tiverton Gazette and East Devon Herald

Figure 53. Reverend Rossiter Ireland (Rector 1857-1908)

Appendix 1

Rectors of Sampford Peverell

Date	Name	By whom presented
27 March 1278	Richard de Bath	Sir Hugh Peverell Kt
8 July 1324	Richard de Esse	Sir Eli Cotel Kt
8 February 1341	John Hurne de Foulders	Sir Oliver de Dynham
5 May 1349	John Barron	Sir Oliver de Dynham
31 January 1361	Simon Yem	Lady Joan de Dynham (relict of Sir Oliver)
1 June 1390	William Rolle	Lady Joan de Dynham (relict of Sir Oliver)
27 August 1430	William Colles	Margaret Duchess of Clarence
19 July 1455	William Daverell	Duke of Richmond
1 October 1470	Jacob Molyneux	Duke of Richmond
15 December 1489	Thomas Evyes	Margaret Countess of Richmond & Derby
7 March 1501	William Bowres	Margaret Countess of Richmond & Derby
13 January 1531	John Stryngar	Duke of Richmond
8 February 1533	Robert West	Duke of Richmond
4 March 1540	John Powlett	Sir Hugh Powlett Kt
16 August 1565	John Wolton	Sir Amias Powlett Kt
23 September 1571	Lewis Swete	Sir Amias Powlett Kt
17 February 1579	Lawrence Bodlye (1) (2)	Sir Amias Powlett Kt
7 August 1584	Francis Pownall	Sir Amias Powlett Kt
20 April 1586	Emmanuel Massie MA	Sir Amias Powlett Kt
20 July 1633	Thomas Collins MA	Rt.Hon. John Lord Powlett
25 July 1665	Christopher Coward MA	Rt.Hon. John Lord Powlett
10 June 1668	John Gawler MA	Rt.Hon. John Lord Powlett
5 August 1697	George Drake MA	Rt.Hon. John Lord Powlett
8 December 1741	Bertie Henley MA (3)	John, Earl Powlett, Viscount & Baron Hinton
23 September 1760	John Adney MD (3)	John, Earl Powlett, Viscount & Baron Hinton
20 June 1815	Simon Pidsley MA (3)	Reverend Simon Pidsley
21 November 1821	Richard Skinner BA (3)	John Silifant of Colebroke & Thos.Hugo of Crediton
11 February 1835	Edward Pidsley BA	John Silifant of Colebroke & Thos.Hugo of Crediton
22 November 1847	Anthony Boulton DD	Reverend Edward Pidsley
10 August 1854	William Blake Doveton MA	Reverend Edward Pidsley
4 March 1857	George W Rossiter Ireland LLD MA	Trustees of Mrs Mary Eliza Ireland
7 December 1908	Philip Rossiter	"Keble College,Oxford"
20 February 1911	John James Rees	"Keble College,Oxford"
27 June 1940	Joseph George Brunskill	"Keble College,Oxford"

18 November 1944	Matthew Ernest Coyle (4)	"Keble College,Oxford"
15 December 1962	John Newton Hardy	Bishop of Exeter
21 January 1967	Arthur Basil Nelson (5)	"Keble College,Oxford"
8 February 1983	Ivor Frank Marsh	The Sampford Peverell Patronage Board
6 December 1985	Michael Charles Boyes (6)	The Sampford Peverell Patronage Board
6 August 1993	Brian Petty	The Sampford Peverell Patronage Board
1 September 1999	Keith Gale (7)	Appointed as Acting Rector by the Bishop of Exeter

Figure 54. Reverend Keith Gale (Acting Rector since 1999)

Notes:

1. Also known as 'Bodley', he is the first Rector to be given the title of 'Reverend' in the Parish records

2. Lawrence Bodlye was the brother of Canon Bodlye of Exeter, who founded theBodleian Library in Oxford.

3. The living of Sampford Peverell was combined with Uplowman from 1697 to 1835

4. The living of Sampford Peverell was held in plurality with Uplowman from 1951.

5. The Team Ministry of Sampford Peverell was established in 1976 with the addition of Holcombe Rogus and Burlescombe

6. Halberton with Ash Thomas, Hockworthy and Huntsham were added to the Team Ministry in 1988.

7. Huntsham was informally transferred to the Bampton Team Ministry in 2000 but remains on the Diocesan list of the Sampford Peverell Team.

In praise of Sampford Peverell stained glass windows*

Pevsner's survey of Devon informs us that Sampford Peverell's 'complete set of high quality 19th century glass' was designed and installed between 1861 and 1864 by Lavers, Barraud and Westlake. The windows mostly depict scenes from the life of Christ, but surprisingly Pevsner makes no reference to Saint John the Baptist, who is central to two of them. The formality of a Victorian glazier's art helps us to decipher some of the personalities depicted in these windows. Christ is shown with a red and white halo, whilst each of the apostles has a different single colour and the Virgin Mary is always dressed in blue. Thus, once you have identified the image of a particular individual, it should be possible to find them in the remaining windows, even though the facial images sometimes differ.

Starting with the glorious East End triple light, right at the top one can see three small round lights with the Coat of Arms of the Diocesan Bishop of Exeter on the left and the Royal Coat of Arms on the right. The main window incorporates three scenes. At the top is the Ascension in company with the eleven apostles and the Virgin Mary: Matthias was not appointed in place of Judas until after this event. In the centre there is the traditional scene of the Crucifixion with Mary and John, the disciple whom Jesus loved, and the Centurion Longinius. Finally at the foot we have the Last Supper with a shadowy Judas on the left stealing away from the company.

The remaining three Sanctuary and Chancel windows provide an historical sequence of the life of Christ. Each has four scenes in the blue patterned framework that can be seen in the Nave. Clockwise from the Pulpit the first depicts Jesus' birth and early childhood with the Nativity, the adoration of the Magi, the flight into Egypt and Jesus at the age of 12 talking to the Elders. In the second, nearest the east end of the north wall, there are four familiar scenes from Jesus' Ministry. In the first he is shown welcoming children, referring to the very familiar quotation from St. Mark's Gospel 'Suffer the little children to come unto me and forbid them not.' Next is the raising of Lazarus from the dead, then Mary Magdalene washing his feet and finally Jesus walking on the water, which is also featured in both St. Matthew's and St. Mark's Gospels following their description of the 'feeding of the five thousand'. Finally the third window on the south side of the Sanctuary shows four scenes from the Passion: the Garden of Gethsemane, Jesus carrying his cross on the road to Golgotha, the scourging of Jesus following Pilate's decision to deliver him for crucifixion and lastly the Resurrection.

The first of the Nave windows beside the Pulpit is hard to interpret, as it appears to have no theme to it. Our Lord is shown teaching in the Temple in the bottom left hand panel with an Angel in the panel above him. It is possible that the Reverend Rossiter Ireland gave no clear instructions as there is no particular relationship between these two panels and the two right hand panels that feature apostolic healing. The central Nave window, beside the north door, is devoted to John the Baptist and is one of the two most important windows of this Church. (Fig. 55) The four scenes are not in sequence since his death is depicted at the top. The bottom left hand panel reminds us that according to St. Luke's Gospel Zacharias and Elizabeth could not have children until the angel appeared to Zacharias and told him that he would have a son, who was to be called John. John the Baptist, as he became known, was a renowned preacher and prophet, whose ministry probably took place between 27 and 30 AD, during which time he baptised Jesus in the River Jordan – as shown in the bottom right hand panel. John's preaching was primarily directed against social injustice and religious hypocrisy, which understandably made him many enemies in high places. In particular his denunciation of Herod Antipas, the ruler of Galilee, who was one of the three sons

Figure 55. Saint John the Baptist window - Nave north wall   (Julia Claxton)

of Herod the Great and who had married his brother's wife Herodias, led inevitably to his imprisonment. According to the well known story in St. Matthew's Gospel, Herodias's daughter Salome having danced before Herod was granted a wish. At her mother's behest she chose the execution of Saint John the Baptist and had his head brought to her on a platter. This episode is shown in the top two panels.

While it is quite apparent that the first two of the three Nave windows form part of the patterned sequence that stems from the Chancel, it is quite obvious that the window nearest the organ is of a different design. Although records show it was commissioned and installed at the same date as the others, there is no explanation why this picture of Sampford Peverell's Patron Saint differs in style from the rest. The window has only one picture and no frame although there is a patterned lower panel and it shows Saint John the Baptist preaching, preparing the way for the coming of Jesus.

In the Aisle, which was added by Margaret Beaufort at the end of 15th century, the east end window (the subject of major restoration work in 1997) is of supreme historical importance (Fig. 56), being a very rare example of a window that shows Heaven and Hell-fire together. It is dominated by the risen Christ, supported on

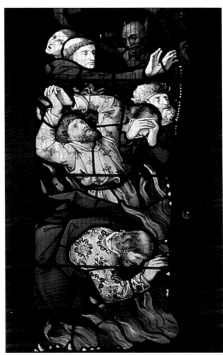

Figure 56. 'Heaven and Hellfire' window - Lady Chapel South Aisle east wall   *(Julia Claxton)*

each side by five apostles together with the Virgin Mary on the left and John the Baptist on the right. The obvious question, "why only ten of the eleven apostles?", is answered in the bottom left hand corner where St. Peter is shown with the Keys to the Kingdom. In the centre is St. Michael, with the Scales of Justice, and in the right hand corner, hell-fire consumes those whose sins have sentenced them to be condemned. It is a very dramatic window, probably one of only three in the country, now seen in all its glory, but which for many years was partially hidden by the Lady Chapel curtain.

The Perpendicular architectural style of the four windows of the Aisle provides much wider openings than the Early English lights in the Nave and Chancel, which had been created 150 years earlier. The artist glazier therefore had scope for a broader canvas and took advantage of their size to provide dramatic images using the considerable amount of light that streams in from this south facing wall. The windows are all devoted to events from the Old Testament instead of the New. At the time only two of these windows were glazed with stained glass, the two windows nearest the Porch being left with clear glass. The first of them, at the eastern end, illustrates the two most well-known stories from the Book of Daniel. In the lower part of the window, on the left, King Nebuchadnezzar is witnessing Shadrach, Meshach and

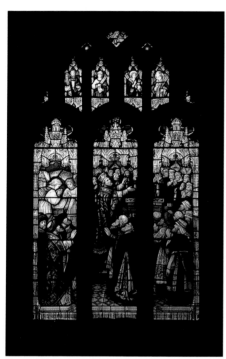

Figure 57. Memorial window Reverend Rossiter Ireland - South Aisle south wall *(Di Cowan)*

Abednego, the three Jews who refused to worship the golden image, emerge unscathed from the burning fiery furnace. Above them is the Prophet Daniel himself, in the lion's den because (later in his life) he had refused to worship Darius the new King. Punished for his insolence, he too emerged unscathed. The second of these Old Testament windows pictures Elijah, with events from the First and Second Book of Kings. In the upper part of this window the Prophet is shown ascending into Heaven in a Chariot of Fire to the admiration of his successor Elisha. Beneath this evocative image the window is divided into three panels, on the left Elijah is being fed by the Ravens, in the centre he is being fed by an angel in the wilderness and on the right he is anointing Jehu as King of Israel.

It is possible that in 1864, when the remaining windows were being re-glazed, the third window in the Aisle still retained some of the early 16th century glazing that was known to have been installed when it was completed and that is the reason why this is the only window without Victorian glass. It was still in situ in one of the Aisle windows at the start of the 19th century but presumably like everything else in this church at that time was in a poor state. Suffice to say that in 1910 this window was re-glazed as a memorial dedicated to the Church's benefactor, the Reverend Rossiter Ireland, who had died in 1908 (Fig. 57). It shows King Solomon at the dedication of the Temple in all its golden glory. The last of these Aisle windows, nearest to the South Porch and entrance to the Church, is also a memorial but was installed by Rossiter Ireland at the end of his Sampford Peverell ministry. It is dedicated to Bishop Henry Philpott of Exeter, who had died in 1869. It shows Moses striking water from the rock and Elijah calling on the wind to produce fire for the sacrifice to Baal at Mount Carmel.

* This Appendix re-prints the text (with minor amendments) of a talk given by Charles Scott-Fox at a special fund-raising service in 1999, which was published in the Parish Magazine and has also been available from the Church Bookstall.

Appendix 3

The Sampford Peverell Ring of Bells

The inscriptions of the Bells and their diameters are as follows:

Treble   TO CALL CHRIST'S FLOCK: 1: ALOUD DO SING: T: B: F: 1761 (shell)
31.5 inches diameter

Second   THOMAS BILBIE CULLOMPTON CAST US AL 1761 (shell)
33.125 inches diameter

Third   MR: F: S: & MR: H: S: CH: WARDENS: T: BIBIE FECIT 1761 (shell)
34.25 inches diameter

Fourth   MR FRANCIS SURRAGE & MR HUGH SWEETLAND
CHURCH WARDENS 1761 (shell)
37.5 inches diameter

Fifth   G MEARS & CO. FOUNDERS LONDON (shell)
ALL GLORY TO GOD
THIS BELL WAS RECAST BY THE JOINT SUBSCRIPTION OF
THE RECTOR AND PARISHIONERS A.D.1863
REVD. G W R IRELAND M A RECTOR
J. BEEDELL   CHURCH WARDENS
W. PAYNE (waist)
43.125 inches diameter

Tenor   MEARS & STAINBANK, FOUNDERS, LONDON (shell)
IN HONOUR OF THE MOST HOLY TRINITY
AND IN PIOUS MEMORY OF
SARAH ELEANOR RENDALL WHO
LIES BURIED IN THE CHANCEL
THIS BELL IS HUMBLY PRESENTED
TO THE TOWER OF THE CHURCH BY
HER BROTHER, THE REVD.
G.W.R. IRELAND, L.L.D. RECTOR, A.D. 1869
ALL THY WORKS PRAISE THEE, O LORD
AND THEY SAINTS GIVE THANKS UNTO THEE (waist)
46.875 inches diameter

Appendix 4

Applicants for meeting house licences

Eleven licences have survived for Sampford and they are most important sources of history. The names of the applicants are given below with the date of their application.

WESLEYAN

9th December 1793 for Samuel Jennings' kitchen. William Hellyer, Joseph Jennings, Richd. Jennings, Samuel Jennings, William Webber.

19th December 1793 for Robert Webber's kitchen. Jno. Webber, John Webber, Robert Webber, William Webber.

19th November 1800 for Francis Taylor's former kitchen. Nicholas Curwood, Samuel Jennings, Frans. Taylor.

1st October 1802 for a newly erected house belonging to trustees. Joseph Algar (Wesleyan minister) Benj. Bale, Henry Cadbury, Nics. Curwood, Wm. Hellyer, Wm. Hellyer (another), Thos. Houze, Samuel Jennings, John Pulman.

29th June 1807 for Samuel Jennings' house. John Clarke, Francis Col[l]ier (Wesleyan minister), William Hellyer, Samuel Jennings (Schoolmaster).

13th October 1817 for George Hellyer's house. William Baker (Wesleyan minister), George Hellyer (Grocer).

BAPTIST

8th July 1799 For John Helier's [sic] house. Thomas Hatch, Danl. Sprague, John Helier.

15th January 1805 For the house of Catherine Webber. Benjamin Thomas, John Stradling, Thos. Martin.

25th May 1806 For "...a house built called the Baptist Chapel .. in the town ... " Benjamin Thomas, Richd. Thomas, Thomas Martin, John Stradling.

BIBLE CHRISTIAN

These licences hint at a mission situation in which there was no real initiative from the local people, so the minister sent to the area had to attend to the business of finding and licensing places for worship.

21st February 1832 For the house of John Goffin. Matthew Robins of Roche in Cornwall (BC Minister).

4th October 1851 for a BC chapel. James Hinks of Tiverton (BC Minister).

Appendix 5

Ecclesiastical census 1851

In 1851 the Government extended the Census of Population to include places of worship, asking for the size of congregation at each service on Sunday March 30th 1851. Questions were also asked about the size and date of the building. The returns from Sampford are summarised below (See Wickes, 1990). The numbers of Sunday school children at the services are given in brackets after the number of adult worshippers on 30th March. The only return to estimate the average congregation was from the Bible Christians.

CHURCH OF ENGLAND
St John's. Erected about 1200.
200 seats.
Congregations: morning 110 (25), afternoon 120 (25)
Signed: [not given]

WESLEYAN METHODIST
Erected 1803. 156 seats.
Congregations: morning 140 (60), evening 170 (30)
Signed: "George Hellyer, chapel steward, of Sampford Peverell draper and grocer"

BIBLE CHRISTIAN
Erected "Not known but believe before 1800".
Congregations: afternoon 12, evening 31.
Average congregation over past 6 months: afternoon 30, evening 30.
Remarks "This chapel was not opened for public worship for nearly two years but were [sic] reopened about 6 months since so I have only given the average for that period."
Signed: "Richard Harris, manager, of Sampford Peverell"

Appendix 6

Trustees of Sampford Methodist Chapel

The trustees of Sampford Chapel are only a few of the faithful people who have worshipped and worked in the chapel over the years but the names of most of the others are lost to us. In earlier years being a trustee meant a possible financial liability and people of some means were often chosen. There was a leavening of Trustees from local chapels and one or two from away who had Sampford connections. These lists are of particular value as they indicate the social background of the trustees and thus of the congregations at different periods. The 1820 list is given here; later lists can be found in Thorne 1993.

The Trustees named in the 1820 Deed for the Chapel and its site and Candy's House

John Cowlen (SP; Gentleman),

John Curwood (SP; Staymaker),

Thomas Curwood (Huntspill, Somerset; Shopkeeper),

Joseph Davey (Cullompton; Cloth Merchant),

George Hellyer (SP; Shopkeeper),

Richard House (Halberton; Yeoman),

Samuel Jennings (Rotherhithe, Surrey; Esquire),

Thomas Langford Pannell (SP; Schoolmaster),

Robert Loosemore (SP; Yeoman),

John Prickman (SP; Shopkeeper),

Joseph Sanders (Tiverton; Gent.),

Thomas Tapper (SP; Saddler),

William Row (SP; Gentleman),

John Veness (Burlescombe; Shopkeeper),

William Wawman (SP; Shopkeeper).

Statistics of Methodist membership at Sampford

These numbers are recorded in the circuit schedules and are for the September/October quarterly meeting where available. They are formal church memberships; congregations were bigger.

WESLEYAN/METHODIST

1777 19;   1796 04;   1797 07;   1803 13;   1805 15;
1810 22;   1820 28;   1830 22;   1840 35;   1850 40;   1860 22;   1870 20;
1880 16;   1890 22;   1900 14;   1910 16;   1920 14;   1930 20;   1940 14;
1950 12;   1960 15;   1965 14;   1993 19;

BIBLE CHRISTIAN

1842 04;   1845 13;   1850 01;   1855 08;   1860 15;   1865 07;   1870 02;